Merry Christmas 1997

John &

Nancy Love Karen

MEXICAN MAIN DISHES

★ ★ ★ ★ ★

MEXICAN MAIN DISHES

TORTILLAS, TAMALES, FAJITAS, ENCHILADAS, AND MORE!

MARLENA SPIELER

CHARTWELL
BOOKS, INC.

A QUINTET BOOK

Published by Chartwell Books
A Division of Book Sales, Inc.
114 Northfield Avenue,
Edison, New Jersey 08837
This edition produced for sale in the U.S.A., its
territories and dependencies only.

ISBN 0-7858-0383-1

This book was designed and produced by
Quintet Publishing Limited
6 Blundell Street
London N7 9BH

Creative Director: Richard Dewing
Designer: Ian Hunt
Project Editor: Stefanie Foster
Text Editor: Diana Vowles
Illustrator: Joanne Makin

Typeset in Great Britain by
Central Southern Typesetters, Eastbourne
Manufactured by C. H. Colour Scan Sdn. Bhd., Malaysia
Printed by Star Standard Industries (Pte) Ltd, Singapore

ACKNOWLEDGEMENTS

A warm thank you to those who sampled my recipes, enjoying the successes and good-naturedly putting up with the dishes that didn't quite make it. To my daughter Leah for her continual enthusiasm for the pleasures of the table, especially the Mexican table. To my step-daughter Gretchen, with whom I have shared many late-night carnitas quesadillas picnics; to my husband Alan McLaughlan for his stamina and creative shopping; to Peter Milne for his appreciation and delicious food ideas; to Jon Harford for his vegetarian sensibility in recipe testing; to Hoops and everyone at Outdoor Chef, where the grilled and barbecued dishes were tested on the marvellous gas barbecue.

Jerome Freeman and Sheila Hannon, Amanda Hamilton and Tim Hemmeter, Christine and Maureen Smith, Nigel and Graham, Esther Novack and John Chendo, Fiona Beckett, Kathleen Griffen, Sheila Dillon, Kamala Friedman, Sandy Waks, Trish Robinson, Michelle Schmidt, Simon Parkes, Michael Bauer, M.A. and Richard Mariner for the tortilla press,

Paula Levine for the tortillas, Jill Vaux, Vanessa Welch, Etty and Bruce Blackman, Paul Richardson, Susan Redgrave, Helene and Robin Simpson, the Wight family, Lena Gilbert and Jason Gaber all tucked in to various dishes and helped in the testing, even if they weren't aware of it at the time. Thanks to Jackie Higuera McMahan, for her company one lovely afternoon in San Francisco's Mission District. Thanks, too, to my lovely cat Freud, though having a cat who insists his food bowl is garnished with fresh coriander and accompanied by tortillas is as annoying as it is amusing.

Thanks to my parents, Caroline and Izzy Smith, Aunt Estelle and Uncle Sy Opper, and Grandmother Sophia Dubowsky who whetted my appetite for Mexican food when I was young and vulnerable to this delicious life-long addiction.

And to Stefanie Foster and Quintet Publishing for commissioning me to write this book.

CONTENTS

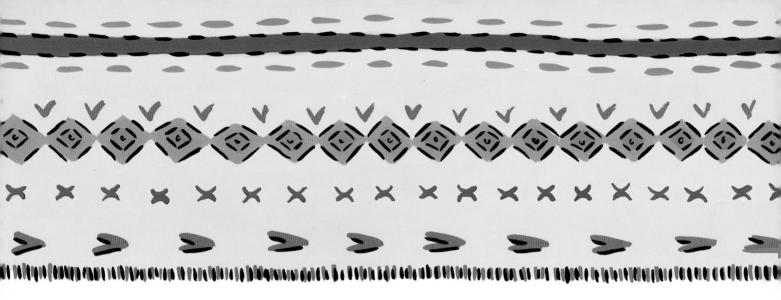

INTRODUCTION

Sitting down to the *comida corrida*, or main meal, in Mexico is one of the great moments of each day, for what could be more enticing than great platters of this hearty, usually spicy, food?

While the meal begins with soup, or antojitos or botonas, it is the main courses that form the real meal. You might find a simmering cazuela of chicken and vegetables, perfumed with spices and colored with bright red chili purée, or a potful of meats and vegetables, such as turkey mole, to be eaten as both the soup and main course.

Often dinner will be cooked on the grill to give smoky, succulent, and irresistible flavors and textures. You might find strips of beef (fajitas), golden marinated chicken, brick-hued fish, all spicy morsels meant to be rolled up in an exquisitely fresh tortilla.

A main course Mexicana might also consist of a deep tureen of robust soup such as posole, rich with starchy hominy and meaty chunks of pork, its salady garnish providing a fresh contrast, or a casserole filled with enchiladas, or chilaquiles (tortillas layered and baked with chili sauces into a savory delectable mush.) Paella, roasted meats or poultry, braised fish – all may be the main plate.

This book is full of such main courses, or *platillos fuertes*, from that vast and fascinating land. From the lush tropical reaches of the Yucatan to the northern arid plains of Sonora and the beaches and vineyards of Baja, each region is represented by its own distinctive flavors and perfumes.

NOTE: While none of the recipes are difficult there are several somewhat unusual cooking techniques that form a particular culinary language. Once you are familiar with the processes you will find them easy.

- Puréeing sauces then "frying" in a small amount of oil until the mixture intensifies, before adding stock and other ingredients.

- Toasting and roasting vegetables such as onions, tomatoes, garlic, and chilis, before puréeing into sauces.

- Toasting and grinding dried chilis into powders.

- Toasting, soaking, and puréeing dried chilis into sauces.

GLOSSARY

CHILIS

Capsicum frutescens, otherwise known as chilis, or hot peppers, come in so wide a variety they are nearly impossible to categorize. However, there are some basic guidelines to help us with the chilis that are more easily available outside of Mexico.

> WHENEVER USING CHILIS, TAKE CARE. WASH YOUR HANDS IMMEDIATELY AFTER USING, AND DO NOT TOUCH YOUR EYES OR OTHER SENSITIVE AREAS AS THE VOLATILE OILS LINGER AND LINGER. TO PREVENT YOUR HANDS FROM BURNING FOR DAYS AFTER HANDLING CHILIS, USE RUBBER GLOVES.
>
> WHEN HEATING CHILIS IN A PAN, OR WHIRLING THEM IN A BLENDER OR FOOD PROCESSOR, DO NOT INHALE OR PLACE YOUR FACE NEAR THE LID WHEN REMOVING IT. INHALING CHILI FUMES CAN BE VERY PAINFUL AND DISTRESSING. CHILDREN ARE PARTICULARLY SUSCEPTIBLE AND SHOULD NOT BE IN THE SAME ROOM WITH FRYING CHILIS.

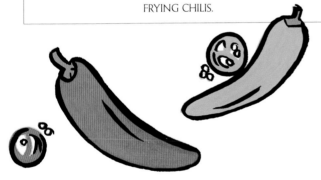

Chilis come fresh or dried. Fresh they are bright and full flavored, most often available in green, but red and sometimes yellow varieties are also found. Generally, with a few explosive exceptions, the smaller the chili the hotter.

Tiny Thai, or bird's eye chilis are very very hot, serranos on the hotter side of medium, while the larger Kenya, or jalapeño, are hot but not impossible. The jalapeño type chilis are probably the most useful all-purpose chili, for their pleasant flavor and bearable heat. The poblano chili looks much like a

regular green bell pepper and is on the milder side as chilis go; it is lovely for stuffing. The most widely available exception to the "small is hottest" rule is the Scots bonnet, a lantern shaped chili in parrot-like hues of red, yellow, green, and orange that is breathtakingly, aggressively hot. This is one of the most readily available of chilis, and care should be taken to acclimatize yourself to its tropical heat.

Fresh green chilis may be used raw, cooked, or roasted, then added to sauces, stews, etc.

Dried chilis come in a wide range of types such as pasilla, ancho, guajillo, puya, cascabel, and so on. These are the chilis used to make "mild chili powder". To make your own mild chili powder lightly toast whichever chili you desire, then cut off the stems and remove the seeds. Cut the lightly toasted chili into small pieces and whirl in a coffee grinder until it forms a powder. Storebought mild chili powder may be mixed with paprika and used in place of the individual chilis in sauces.

CHIPOTLE CHILI

This is the dried, smoked jalapeño, fiery hot and scented with smoke. It is available dried or in tins, "en adobo", a spicy marinade. A recipe for chipotles en adobo is in the Salsa chapter.

JALAPEÑOS EN ESCABECHE

These pickled chilis are delicious with refried beans and cheese, or tucked into any taco or torta. Widely available.

TOMATILLOS

Green husk tomatoes with a sour flavor and a crisp texture. They must be husked and blanched before using, as raw they are not so delightful as when tender and ready to be puréed into sauces. Since they add a tart accent, occasionally unsweetened gooseberries or a handful of shredded sorrel, or a big squeeze of lemon and a few underripe tomatoes can take their place.

NOPALES

Cactus pads, an unusual green vegetable doted on throughout Mexico. Must be peeled and blanched first to rid them of their sticky juices (much like okra). Occasionally available fresh in West Indian markets; imported from Mexico in tins. If unavailable, use blanched green beans tossed with a few drops of vinegar, onion, and oregano.

SOME MEXICAN COOKING METHODS

ROASTING AND PEELING CHILIS

Place chilis of any sort over a flame and cook, lightly charring the skin, turning until evenly charred. If using small chilis, place them in an ungreased skillet instead or skewer them before placing on flame. When evenly and lightly charred, place in a plastic bag or in the bottom of a saucepan. Seal the bag or place the lid on the pan and leave for 30–60 minutes. Remove and use a paring knife to peel off the skin. Cut off and discard the stem and remove the seeds.

TOASTING GARLIC AND ONIONS

Place unpeeled garlic cloves in a heavy ungreased skillet and cook over medium heat until cloves char lightly and turn soft inside; turn several times so that they cook evenly. Remove from pan. To use, squeeze from skin. Use the cooked flesh and discard the skin. Onions may be toasted by cutting them unpeeled (or peeled, as desired) in half, then placing the cut pieces on an ungreased pan and cooking over medium heat until charred. Remove and use the flesh as desired.

REHYDRATING CHILIS

Lightly toast dried chilis by holding them over a flame or tossing them in a heavy ungreased pan over medium low heat. Place in a bowl and cover with boiling water. Let sit 30–45 minutes until chilis are soft, then either purée and sieve, or scrape away the flesh from the papery skin (which should then be discarded).

MASHING GARLIC

To extract full flavor from garlic, use a mortar and pestle; add a dash of salt before crushing.

ROASTING TOMATOES

Place tomatoes in a baking dish and drizzle with oil and salt. Bake in a medium hot oven for 45 minutes or until they shrink and concentrate in flavor. Let cool in their juices then remove skins and squeeze to extract the flavorful juices in the skins. Discard squeezed out skins and combine with the flesh of the tomatoes and with the pan juices. Tomatoes may also be toasted, using the technique described for onions and garlic.

CHAPTER ONE

TORTILLAS, BEANS, AND SALSAS

★ ★ ★ ★ ★

TORTILLAS, BEANS, AND SALSAS

Along with rice, tortillas and beans form the basics of the Mexican kitchen. Most everyday meals are based on those foods, along with a bowl of salsa to spice it up, whatever vegetables the garden or market may yield, and perhaps some braised, simmered or broiled meat, poultry, or fish.

CORN TORTILLAS

Fresh tortillas are the basis of Mexican cuisine: the flat cakes of pounded lime-slaked corn have a distinctive flavor and texture like no other food I know. Tortillas are not only the bread of Mexico, they are the plates and knives and forks as well. Tortillas wrap up tacos and enchiladas, and are served with barbecues, for impromptu tacos. They are served as a snack, or as a bread accompaniment alongside the *comida corrida*, or midday dinner.

**MAKES 12 6INCH TORTILLAS
OR 24 3INCH TORTILLAS**

1lb. masa harina	¾–1 cup water at warm room temperature (less if weather is humid)

1. Mix the flour with the water until it forms a soft but not gummy dough.

2. Take several plastic bags and cut the sides so that each forms a large rectangle. Heat a heavy skillet or comal; I find that using two at a time makes the task quicker.

3. Roll a piece of dough into a ball about 1½inches in diameter; place this ball on one side of a plastic rectangle, then place this rectangle on to the open tortilla press. Cover the other side with a plastic rectangle.

4. Close the press and push the handle down evenly and hard. Open it up and take the tortilla out of the press, picking up the whole thing carefully, then peel off the plastic and plop the tortilla directly into the hot pan. Lightly oiled hands makes the dough easier to handle.

5. Cook each tortilla quickly, about 2 minutes in total. When cooking the first side, wait for the edges to appear dry, then turn over and cook the second side until it is lightly speckled. Turn over and cook the first side a few more moments, then stack on a plate, and keep warm, covered with a clean cloth. Tortillas may puff up as they cook; this is a good sign, indicating a light, well-cooked tortilla.

REHEATING PURCHASED TORTILLAS

1. Lightly spray each tortilla with water and let them rest for a few minutes while you heat a lightly oiled heavy-based skillet.

2. Put the whole stack of tortillas in it. When the bottom tortilla is warm, turn the whole stack using a spatula, so that the bottom tortilla is now the top one.

3. Cover and allow to cook in the steam for a few moments, then repeat, dividing the stack of tortillas from the middle. Each tortilla should be exposed to both the heat of the bottom of the pan and the steam that rises to the top.

4. Remove from the pan, place on a plate and cover with a clean cloth, sides folded over to keep the tortillas soft and warm.

NUTRITIONAL INFORMATION			
	TOTAL FAT	SAT FAT	CHOL	ENERGY
Total	16.5g	0mg	0mg	1840kcals
Per 6"	1.4g	0mg	0mg	153kcals
Per 3–4"	0.7g	0mg	0mg	77kcals

TOSTADAS

Stale tortillas make the crispest tostadas as they absorb less oil in the frying. Tostadas are oil-"toasted" tortillas, crisp as a cracker and very versatile. Whole, a tostada can form the basis for a one-portion dish. Spread with refried beans or sprinkle with cheese and melt the top, and serve with fresh crunchy salad, salsa, and herbs.

LOWER FAT TOSTADAS

Brush stale tortillas with vegetable oil and place on a baking sheet in a preheated oven at 425°F. Bake until crisp and golden and lightly browned in places, about 15 minutes. Alternatively, bake in the oven at 300°F for 45 minutes or so. The long slow bake gives a crisper, more brittle crunch to the tostadas. Remove and place on a dry surface.

TRADITIONAL TOSTADAS

Fry the tortillas, one at a time, in shallow vegetable oil or melted lard or shortening, until crisp and golden-brown. Remove from the pan and drain on paper towels, then place on a dry surface. Keep warm in the oven at 350°F for up to 10 minutes: lower the heat to 275°F if keeping warm for up to 1 hour.

TOTOPOS (TORTILLA CHIPS)

Cut tortillas into wedges and prepare as for Tostadas . Use for chilaquiles, nachos, or for tortilla soup.

FAT-FREE TOTOPOS

Wet the tortillas one at a time and cut into wedges. Sprinkle with salt if desired. Arrange in a single layer on a non-stick baking sheet then baking in a preheated oven at 500°F for 4 minutes. Turn with a spatula or tongs and continue baking until golden-brown and crisp, about 3 minutes.
These will keep in an airtight container for two weeks.

TORTILLAS DE HARINA

FLOUR TORTILLAS

Flour tortillas are slightly chewy, lightly flecked from the pan, and delicious with chilied stews, barbecued meats, or wrapped around frijoles refritos and cheese for a hefty burrito.

MAKES 10-12 8INCH TORTILLAS

| ½ cup lard shortening, or vegetable oil | 1 cup lukewarm water |
| 1lb. all-purpose flour, sifted | 2 tsp. salt |

1. Work the lard or oil into the flour with your fingers or in a food processor until it forms a crumb-like mixture.

2. Mix the water and salt, then stir into the flour.

3. Knead the dough for about 3 minutes until no longer sticky. Cover and set aside for 2 hours or overnight.

4. Knead the dough again, then roll into small balls. For 7inch tortillas make 2inch balls, 14inch tortillas will need balls about 3inch in diameter.

5. Place each ball on a floured board, then roll into a 7inch round, turning the dough so that the round becomes paper-thin.

6. Heat an ungreased heavy-based skillet, griddle or comal until it is very hot. Place a flat dough round on the hot surface. Leave it for 20–30 seconds – if it puffs up, flatten it again with the back of a spatula.

7. Turn and cook on the other side for about 10 seconds. Transfer to a plate and keep covered with a clean cloth while you prepare the rest of the dough. The tortillas should be soft and flexible. To use, reheat on the griddle before filling, etc.

NUTRITIONAL INFORMATION				
	TOTAL FAT	SAT FAT	CHOL	ENERGY
Total	130g	51g	116mg	2819kcals
10–12 8in	13g–11g	5g–4g	12g–10g	282kcals
				235kcals

FRIJOLES

BEANS

Throughout Mexico, a pot sits on each backburner, bubbling away quietly, yielding up its contents of tender beans that accompany nearly every main course and also form fillings for many of the tortilla-based antojitos. The liquid used for cooking beans is added to soups and stews, and is used to cook rice. (Arroz negro, rice cooked in black bean liquor, is startlingly grey in color but very savory and satisfying to eat.) The color, size, and shape of the beans depends on where in Mexico you are. In general, black beans are eaten in the southern, more tropical regions, pink and pinto beans further north. Little white beans are served in the Yucatan, and big lima-like beans in Tarasca.

FRIJOLES REFRITOS

REFRIED BEANS

Despite the name "refried", frijoles refritos is not fried twice – rather it is puréed and heated in a small amount of hot fat, more or less fried once. I have heard it said that it is with typical south-of-the-border exuberance that many things are exaggerated, even the number of times the beans are fried!

SERVES 6 – 8

1 quantity Frijoles de Olla (page 12) made with pinto, pinquito, or other pink beans	3tbsp. vegetable oil
	½tsp. ground cumin
1–2 onions, chopped	½tsp. mild chili powder
	salt

1. Mash or purée the beans to a coarse, chunky consistency. Leave some whole, others in pieces, still others puréed into a thick sauce-like mixture.
2. Fry the onion in the vegetable oil until softened and lightly browned, then sprinkle in the cumin and chili powder.
3. Ladle in a scoop of the bean mixture, cook over medium-high heat until thickened and slightly darkened in color, then add another ladleful of the beans and repeat until all the beans have simmered into a thick, darkened, flavorful mixture.
4. Season with salt to taste.

NUTRITIONAL INFORMATION				
	TOTAL FAT	SAT FAT	CHOL	ENERGY
Total	60g	13g	45mg	2309kcals
Serves 6	10g	2g	8mg	385kcals
Serves 8	7.5g	1.5mg	6mg	289kcals

VARIATION

FRIJOLES REFRITOS CON QUESO

Top refried pinto or other pink beans with about 1½ cups coarsely shredded mild white cheese and either heat in the oven or stir in. Let the cheese melt then serve.

FRIJOLES DE OLLA

SIMMERED BEANS

The green herb epazote, said to help mitigate the embarrassing effects of beans, is usually added to the pot of simmering beans. A leaf or two of mint, while not the same thing, gives a similar flavor and wind-easing result. Use these beans as an accompaniment, to make frijoles refritos, or anywhere simmered beans are called for. A bowl of warm frijoles de olla, along with a few warm tortillas and a chili or two, is the mainstay of the Mexican diet.

FRIJOLES BORRACHOS
DRUNKEN BEANS

SERVES 6 - 8

1 onion, chopped	½–1 fresh green chili such as jalapeño, thinly sliced
3 cloves garlic, chopped	1 cup flavorful beer, or as desired
½ cup diced bacon	1 quantity Frijoles de Olla (page 12)
5 tomatoes, diced	salt and pepper
½ green pepper or mild green chili, coarsely chopped	

1. Place the onion, garlic and bacon in a skillet and slowly fry until the bacon is crisp and onions soft.

2. Add the tomatoes, pepper, and chili and continue to cook until thickened and sauce-like.

3. Purée half the beans with enough of the beer to make a thick sauce.

4. Pour the puréed beans and reserved whole beans into the pan and cook over a high heat, scraping up the bottom so that it doesn't burn and stick, until the beans have cooked into a thick paste, adding a little extra beer as needed. Season with salt and pepper.

SERVES 6 - 8

1lb. pinto (or pinquito, or pink) or black beans, picked over	9–13oz. smoky bacon
2 medium onions, chopped	several mint leaves
1 head of garlic, unpeeled and cut into halves crosswise	salt

1. Soak beans overnight. Alternatively, place the beans in a saucepan with cold water to cover. Bring to a boil, cook for a few minutes, then remove from the heat. Let sit, covered, for 1 hour. The beans should have plumped up and softened somewhat, absorbing quite a bit of water in the process.

2. Add the onion, garlic, bacon, and mint to the pan and add water to cover.

3. Bring to a boil then reduce the heat to low and simmer uncovered, stirring once or twice, for 1½–2 hours, or until the beans are softened.

4. Add salt to taste.

NUTRITIONAL INFORMATION

	TOTAL FAT	SAT FAT	CHOL	ENERGY
Total	27g	9g	45mg	1969kcals
Serves 6	4.5g	1.5g	8mg	328kcals
Serves 8	3g	1g	6mg	246kcals

NUTRITIONAL INFORMATION

	TOTAL FAT	SAT FAT	CHOL	ENERGY
Total	38g	13g	68mg	2350kcals
Serves 6	6g	2g	11mg	392kcals
Serves 8	4.5g	1.5g	8mg	294kcals

SALSAS AND SPICE MIXTURES

Salsas are the gastronomical soul of Mexican food. The simplest dish – a bowl of rice, a boiled egg, or a chunk of fish – is elevated to superb by the addition of a zesty, chili-spiced salsa. Salsa can be as simple as chopped tomatoes, onions, and chilis. One of the most breathtakingly delicious salsas I ever tasted was chopped cilantro and green chilis, enlivened with a bit of garlic and a squirt of lime. Fresh fruit makes a refreshing salsa, its sweet, juicy flavor a balance for the fiery chili pepper. Proprietary brands of salsa can be excellent; the best are from Mexico. I am fond of El Yucateca and Bufala Brand Chipotle salsa.

SALSA CRUDA
UNCOOKED SALSA
WITH GARLIC AND TOMATO

This is a classic salsa, rich with garlic, parsley, and cilantro. For a chunky salsa leave it as it is; for a smooth purée, give it a whirl in the blender for a moment.
Enjoy dabbed on to nearly anything, even just a swipe on a fresh corn tortilla or a spoonful alongside a bowl of rice.

SERVES 4

3 cloves garlic, chopped

2 jalapeño or serrano chilis, chopped

½ onion, chopped

1lb. flavourful raw tomatoes, chopped

2–3tbsp. chopped fresh parsley

2–3tbsp. chopped fresh cilantro

salt and ground cumin to taste

juice of 1 lime

1. Combine all the ingredients and taste for seasoning. Keeps 4–5 days in the refrigerator.

NUTRITIONAL INFORMATION				
	TOTAL FAT	SAT FAT	CHOL	ENERGY
Total	1.5g	0.5g	0mg	108kcals
Per Serving	0.4g	0.1g	0mg	27kcals

SALSA FRIA
HOT TOMATO SALSA
WITH VINEGAR

SERVES 4

1 cup chunky tomato juice (use either crushed fresh ripe tomatoes or tinned tomatoes coarsely chopped, and their juice)

1 green onion, thinly sliced

3–5 or more very hot small thin chilis such as cayenne or Thai

1 clove garlic, chopped

¼–⅓ cup water

large dash of oregano

large dash of ground cumin or crushed toasted cumin seeds

salt

2–3tbsp. vinegar

small dash of sugar (optional)

1. Combine all ingredients and let rest for at least 30 minutes to develop the flavors. Keeps up to 1 week in the refrigerator.

NUTRITIONAL INFORMATION				
	TOTAL FAT	SAT FAT	CHOL	ENERGY
Total	0.38g	0.01g	0mg	57kcals
Per Serving	0.09g	0g	0mg	14kcals

SALSA DE PINA
PINEAPPLE SALSA

S E R V E S   4

¾–1 cup pineapple juice

1 clove garlic, chopped

1 green onion, thinly sliced

1 ripe tomato, finely chopped, or ¼ cup tinned tomato juice or crushed tomatoes

1tbsp. coarsely chopped fresh mint

1tbsp. coarsely chopped cilantro

hot pepper sauce such as Tabasco to taste, or crush a fresh red chili in a mortar and pestle

dash of ground cumin

juice of ½ lime plus a little of the grated zest

salt

dash of sugar

1. Mix the ingredients and let rest for at least 30 minutes to develop the flavors.

NUTRITIONAL INFORMATION				
	TOTAL FAT	SAT FAT	CHOL	ENERGY
Total	0.5g	0.1g	0mg	125kcals
Per Serving	0.15g	0.02g	0mg	31kcals

SALSA CRUDA DE CHIPOTLE
CHIPOTLE-ONION SALSA RELISH

S E R V E S   4

1 chipotle en adobo, plus 1tbsp. of its marinade (from can) or 2 dried chipotle chilis softened with boiling water and left to sit for 30 minutes

2–3 cloves garlic, chopped

1tbsp. vegetable oil

1tsp. chopped fresh cilantro

juice of ½ lemon or lime

dash of allspice or cloves

salt

1. Chop the chipotle chili and combine with the onion, garlic, oil, and cilantro.

2. Season to taste with lemon or lime, allspice or cloves, and salt. Lasts up to 5 days in the refrigerator.

NUTRITIONAL INFORMATION				
	TOTAL FAT	SAT FAT	CHOL	ENERGY
Total	21g	3g	0mg	219kcals
Per Serving	5.5g	0.75g	0mg	55kcals

SALSA VERDE DE TOMATILLOS
TOMATILLO SALSA

This is the basic green salsa, tangy from the slightly sour, fresh-tasting husk tomato, that you will find on tables throughout Mexico and parts of America's Southwest. It is especially good with rich foods such as pork carnitas, or bean and cheese burritos.

S E R V E S   4

14oz. tomatillos, cooked, drained, and puréed

1 onion, chopped

2 cloves garlic, chopped

2 fresh green chilis, chopped, or to taste

2tbsp. chopped fresh cilantro

salt and ground cumin to taste

1. Combine all the ingredients and taste for seasoning. Lasts for up to 5 days in the refrigerator.

NUTRITIONAL INFORMATION				
	TOTAL FAT	SAT FAT	CHOL	ENERGY
Total	0.7g	0.01g	0mg	96kcals
Per Serving	0.2g	0.0g	0mg	24kcals

V A R I A T I O N
SALSA VERDE CON NOPALES
Add 6oz. cooked drained diced cactus (fresh or canned).

T I M E - S A V I N G   V A R I A T I O N
Combine 6oz. cooked, drained, diced cactus with approximately ½ cup purchased salsa verde. Season to taste with salt, pepper, garlic, cumin, and chopped cilantro.

SALSA DE CHILE PASILLA
MILD RED CHILI SAUCE

This is the classic red chili sauce for making enchiladas, or simmering meats, or oomphing up soups or braises. You can omit the tomatoes if you like, or use stock for soaking the chilis for a richer-flavored sauce.

Add this sauce to browned beef or pork as the braising liquid and simmer until tender for an excellent chili rojo con carne, to spoon up in bowlfuls or wrap into tender tortillas for burritos and tacos.

SERVES 4

4 large smooth-skinned dried chilis	8 ripe tomatoes, quartered, or 1¾ cups canned tomatoes
2–3 large crinkly chilis such as ancho, negro, pasilla, etc	¼tsp. ground cumin
2 cups water or stock, hot but not boiling	dash of ground cinnamon
6 cloves garlic, unpeeled	dash of dried thyme
1 onion, peeled and cut into chunks	2–3tsp. sugar
1 clove garlic, chopped	salt
	1tbsp. vegetable oil
	juice of ½ lime, or to taste

1. Lightly toast the chilis over an open flame or in an ungreased heavy-based skillet until they change color.

2. Remove the stems, seeds and veins from the chilis, break the flesh up into little pieces and place in a bowl or saucepan. Pour in the water or stock to cover the chilis and leave, covered, to soften, about 20 minutes. The liquid should be cool enough to touch and the chilis softened and fleshy.

3. Meanwhile, roast the whole garlic cloves and onion chunks in an ungreased pan until lightly charred and the garlic is tender. Remove from the heat. When cool enough to handle, peel the garlic.

4. Chop the garlic and onion and place in a food processor or blender along with the raw chopped garlic, tomatoes, chilis, and enough of the soaking liquid to make a smoothish sauce. When the sauce is smooth whirl in the rest of the soaking liquid and season with cumin, cinnamon, thyme, sugar, and salt. (The sauce may be sieved for a smoother, more digestible texture.)

5. Heat the vegetable oil in a heavy-based pan. When hot, ladle in about half of the chili sauce, cook down for a few minutes then ladle in the rest. Cook for about 10 minutes, or until the sauce thickens a little and concentrates its flavor.

6. Remove from the heat and season with lime, balancing it with the spices, salt, and sugar. Lasts up to 1 week in the refrigerator.

NUTRITIONAL INFORMATION				
	TOTAL FAT	SAT FAT	CHOL	ENERGY
Total	13.5g	2g	0mg	323kcals
Per Serving	3.5g	0.5g	0mg	81kcals

VARIATIONS

All mild chili sauces can be prepared this way. Chilis such as ancho, negro, mulatto, and some pasillas will give a dark, almost chocolatey sauce; light red chilis such as New Mexico, California, guajillo, and some pasillas will give a brighter, lighter red sauce with a brighter, lighter flavor.

SALSA RANCHERA
COOKED TOMATO SAUCE

This all-purpose tomato and pepper sauce can be used to top eggs for huevos rancheros, served with broiled fish and plantains, thinned with stock for soup. The recipe makes about 4½ pints and keeps in the refrigerator for up to a week or in the freezer for up to 2 months (although it will pale when heated and needs to be spiced up with chili pepper upon defrosting).

MAKES 4½ PINTS

2tsp. cumin seeds

3lb. fresh or canned tomatoes, diced

⅓ cup vegetable oil

2–3 small to medium-sized onions, peeled and chopped

4–6 cloves garlic, chopped

1tbsp. dried oregano, crumbled

2–3 small hot dried chilis, crumbled, or 1 large mild green chili, roasted, skinned, and diced

1 green pepper, roasted, skinned, and diced

salt

2–4tbsp. chopped fresh cilantro (optional)

1. Toast the cumin seeds in an ungreased heavy-based pan until fragrant, then crush coarsely. Set aside.

2. Purée the tomatoes and set aside.

3. Fry the onions and garlic until softened, then add the cumin seeds, oregano, chilis, green pepper, and puréed tomatoes.

4. Simmer, stirring often, for about 45 minutes or until the sauce is richly flavored and thickened. Season with salt to taste and add cilantro if desired.

NUTRITIONAL INFORMATION			
	TOTAL FAT	SAT FAT	CHOL	ENERGY
Total	92g	11g	0mg	907kcals

SALSA DE MUCHOS CHILES Y JITOMATE

SALSA OF ROASTED TOMATOES
AND MANY DIFFERENT DRIED RED CHILIS

This salsa bursts with quintessential Mexican flavors and while the tomatoes need to be roasted, the chilis toasted and ground, it is very simple to make.

Serve salsa de mucho chilis with anything cooked over an open fire or barbecue, as well as with simmered meals such as puchero. It is excellent on tortillas, with just about anything rolled up in them.

If you do not have each type of chili, either omit or substitute: a New Mexico or California smooth-skinned red chili could take the place of the guajilla and puya, for example.

SERVES 4

1 cascabel chili	5 ripe red tomatoes, toasted to char evenly on all sides, then cooled
1 dry (not marinated) chipotle chili	1–2 cloves garlic, chopped
1 guajillo chili	½ cup water
1 puya chili	salt

1. Lightly toast the chilis on an ungreased pan until they lighten in colour and slightly puff up.

2. Cool and remove the stems, seeds, and veins. Grind the flesh in a coffee grinder to a coarse powder.

3. Cut the tomatoes into pieces and purée with the garlic, chili powder, and water. Add salt to taste. Lasts up to 5 days in the refrigerator.

NUTRITIONAL INFORMATION				
	TOTAL FAT	SAT FAT	CHOL	ENERGY
Total	1.5g	0.5g	0mg	82kcals
Per Serving	0.4g	0.1g	0mg	21kcals

RECADO ROJO

RED CHILI-CITRUS PASTE

This is an excellent all-purpose seasoning paste. Since it keeps for up to 2 weeks in the refrigerator and freezes up to 2 months, I tend to make a double batch so that I have it ready and on hand.

MAKES ¼–⅓ CUP

2 ancho chilis	dash of grated orange zest
1 New Mexican or California chili	1tbsp. lemon or lime juice
1tsp. cumin seeds	dash of oregano
3 chopped cloves garlic	salt
2tbsp. fresh orange juice	

1. Remove the stems and seeds from the chilis then tear the flesh up into smallish pieces.

2. Lightly toast in an ungreased heavy-based pan until the chilis change color slightly. Do not allow them to burn.

3. Lightly toast the cumin seeds in an ungreased heavy-based pan until they are fragrant and slightly darkened.

4. Grind the chilis and cumin together in a spice grinder, coffee grinder, or food processor until they form a rough, mealy consistency.

5. Combine with the garlic, orange juice and zest, lemon or lime juice, and oregano and purée in a food processor or blender until a smoothish paste is formed. Season with salt to taste.

NUTRITIONAL INFORMATION				
	TOTAL FAT	SAT FAT	CHOL	ENERGY
Total	0.5g	0.03g	0mg	23kcals

TIME-SAVING VARIATION

Instead of whole chilis, use 2tbsp. each ancho and pastilla or New Mexico chili powder. Instead of whole cumin seeds, use ground cumin. Toast both as indicated in the recipe, though it will take only a few seconds as they are already ground.

SALSA VERDE DE TOMATILLO Y CHILI ROJO

GREEN SALSA
WITH RED DRIED CHILI

This tomatillo salsa is especially good with simmered chicken or pork, a pile of warm tortillas alongside, although it goes well with grilled seafood, too.

SERVES 4

½ each: dry chipotle chili, guajillo, cascabel, and puya

1 clove garlic, chopped

1¾ cups tomatillos, cooked, coarsely chopped or puréed

2tbsp. vinegar or to taste

salt to taste

dash of ground cumin (optional)

dash of ground turmeric (optional)

1. Lightly toast the chilis until they change in color, about 5 minutes. Remove the stems and seeds and grind the flesh in a coffee grinder.

2. Combine with the garlic, tomatillos, and vinegar, then season to taste with salt, cumin, and turmeric. Lasts up to 5 days in the refrigerator.

NUTRITIONAL INFORMATION				
	TOTAL FAT	SAT FAT	CHOL	ENERGY
Total	0.5g	0g	0mg	71kcals
Per Serving	0.1g	0g	0mg	18kcals

SALSA DE LIMON Y CILANTRO

CILANTRO AND LIME SALSA

This hot and tangy purée of green cilantro, chilis, and lime is a basic in my kitchen.

SERVES 4

2oz. fresh cilantro, chopped

1–2 green chilis, or more, chopped

juice of 1 lime

3 cloves garlic, chopped

1–2 ripe tomatoes, chopped

½tsp. ground cumin

salt

1. Combine all the ingredients. Lasts 5–7 days in the refrigerator.

NUTRITIONAL INFORMATION				
	TOTAL FAT	SAT FAT	CHOL	ENERGY
Total	0.5g	0.01g	0mg	24kcals
Per Serving	0.1g	0g	0mg	6kcals

ACHIOTE SEASONING

Also called annatto, these small rock-hard seeds have a lemony, almost saffron-scented aroma and flavor, and the ability to color almost anything a bright yellow (achiote is used to dye margarine and butter).

Achiote may be ground dry in a coffee or spice grinder, or simmered in water to cover until softened then pounded flat in a mortar and pestle or puréed in a blender or food processor.

GROUND ACHIOTE

4tbsp. achiote seeds

1. Place in a clean spice or coffee grinder and whirl until a fine powder is formed.

SIMMERED ACHIOTE

Place achiote seeds in a small saucepan with water to cover. Bring to a boil, then reduce the heat and simmer for 30–40 minutes. Let rest overnight, then grind or purée with only just enough liquid to bind it.

Achiote paste may be stored in the freezer for up to 6 months.

ACHIOTE OIL

Heat 3 tbsp. achiote seeds in ⅛–½ cup vegetable oil only until bubbles form around the edge of the saucepan. Let infuse overnight, then strain and discard the seeds. The resulting oil will be yellow-tinted.

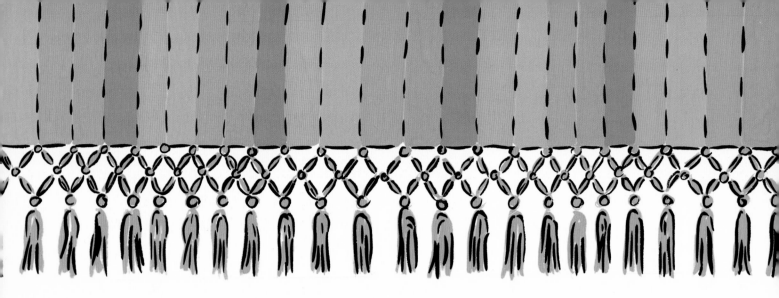

CHAPTER TWO

SIMMERED MEATS, BROTHS, AND TAMALES

★ ★ ★ ★ ★

SIMMERED MEATS, THEIR BROTHS, AND DISHES TO MAKE FROM THEM

A pot of simmering meat or poultry and stock forms the basis of the Mexican kitchen. Many meals begin with soup, then progress to the meat that has simmered in the pot. This is important in a country where poverty is endemic. I've heard it said that roasting is "for the rich! You only get one meal from the pot".

CALDO DE POLLO

CHICKEN STOCK

Instead of using a whole chicken, you can use inexpensive cuts such as wings, necks, or legs.
Simmering chicken with vegetables makes a good flavorful stock to use in other sauces, soups, and stews. It also yields tender moist meat for moles, enchiladas, and so forth.

MAKES 5 PINTS

1 chicken, cut into serving parts	2 bouillon cubes
3-4 carrots, sliced	several sprigs fresh cilantro, chopped
2 onions, chopped	salt and pepper
3-4 cloves garlic, peeled and chopped	

1. Place the chicken, carrots, onions, and garlic in a large pot and fill with water.
2. Bring to a boil. Skim off any scum that develops on the surface as it comes to a boil, then reduce the heat and add the bouillon cubes and cilantro.
3. Simmer covered over a low heat for 1½–2 hours or until the chicken is tender and the stock flavorful.
4. Remove the chicken from the stock and serve as desired.

CALDO DE PUERCO

SIMMERED PORK

AND ITS STOCK

SERVES 4

3-4lb. pork, cut into cubes, or 4-5lb. country-style pork spare ribs	1tsp. ground cumin
1 onion, chopped	1tsp. ground coriander
5 pints water	1tsp. dried oregano
3 cloves garlic, coarsely chopped	2 bay leaves
	1–2 chicken bouillon cubes
	salt and pepper to taste

1. Place the pork, onion, and half the garlic in a large pot of water and bring to a boil. Skim off the scum that forms, then reduce the heat.
2. Add the bouillon cubes. For light stock and meat that is to be cooked a second time, simmer for only 45–60 minutes. For tender meat and rich stock, simmer for about 3 hours.

NUTRITIONAL INFORMATION

	TOTAL FAT	SAT FAT	CHOL	ENERGY
Total	142g	50g	1380mg	2981kcals
Per Serving	35.5g	12.5g	345mg	745kcals

PAVO EN MOLE POBLANO

TURKEY
WITH MOLE SAUCE

The word "mole" comes from the Aztec *molli*, meaning "to grind", and mole sauces, of which there are a near-endless variety, are made from finely ground ingredients, simmered first into a thick paste then thinned and simmered into a glossy smooth sauce. Mole makes a sumptuous filling for tacos, tostadas, enchiladas, and tortillas. This recipe makes a huge potful of mole paste. Since mole improves by making ahead of time it is a marvelous dish for guests, and it freezes beautifully.

½ turkey or 1 chicken, cut into serving pieces

3 bay leaves

1–2 onions, chopped

5 cloves garlic, chopped

3 carrots, diced

handful of fresh cilantro

handful of parsley

2–3 chicken bouillon cubes

MOLE

6–8 ancho chilis

3 mulatto or chilis negro

2–3 pasilla or smooth red chilis such as New Mexico or California

¼tsp. coriander seeds

⅛tsp. black peppercorns

1 inch cinnamon stick

6–8 cloves, the aromatic round part at the head only

½tsp. fennel seeds or anise

5oz. sesame seeds

1lb tomatoes, preferably small flavorful ones

5–8 cloves garlic, unpeeled and whole

1 large onion

½ cup raisins

5–6tbsp. olive oil, lard or shortening

½ cup almonds

4oz. pumpkin seeds

¼ cup peanuts

2 fat slices of French or country bread (about 2–3oz.), cut into bite-sized cubes

2 stale tortillas, cut into strips or bite-sized pieces

4–6tbsp. red or white wine vinegar

1½oz. semi-sweet chocolate

2–3 cups chicken stock, or as needed

salt and pepper to taste

TO SERVE

warmed tortillas

chopped green onions and/or chopped fresh cilantro

thinly sliced cabbage

sour cream (optional)

lime wedges

1. Combine the turkey or chicken with the bay leaves, onions, garlic, and carrots, in a huge pot and fill it with water. Bring to a boil, then skim off the scum that forms at the top.

2. Add cilantro, parsley, and bouillon cubes and reduce the heat, then simmer, covered, for about 3 hours or until the broth is flavorful and the meat very tender. Set aside. Use this stock (caldo de guajalote), for the mole, and also for soups.

3. Meanwhile, make the mole. Lightly toast the chilis on an ungreased skillet until they change color slightly.

4. Tear the chilis into pieces then place in a bowl and cover with boiling water. Cover the bowl and leave to soften for about 20 minutes, turning once or twice to be sure they are evenly soaked.

5. Lightly toast the coriander seeds, peppercorns, cinnamon stick, cloves, fennel seeds or anise, and about two-thirds of the sesame seeds in the skillet. When fragrant, remove to a spice or coffee grinder and whirl to grind. Remove any pieces of hard, large spices such as cinnamon that are left. Set the spice mixture aside.

6. Broil the tomatoes, garlic, and onion until charred on the outside and softened inside. Set aside. When cool dice the tomatoes and onions, then remove the garlic skins and chop the garlic flesh.

7. Fry the raisins in 1tbsp. of oil until they plump up. Set aside.

8. In the same pan, toast the almonds, pumpkin seeds, and peanuts, cooking until the pumpkin seeds sputter and pop. Remove from the heat, then grind in the spice or coffee grinder. Set aside.

9. Add 1–2tbsp. of oil to the pan and lightly brown the bread and tortillas. Remove from the heat and set aside.

10. Remove the stems and seeds from the soaked chilis and purée with half the charred tomatoes, onion, and garlic in a blender or food processor.

11. Heat 2tbsp. oil in a skillet then ladle the chili-tomato mixture into it. Cook over medium heat until concentrated and paste-like.

12. In a blender or food processor, purée the remaining tomatoes, onions, and garlic with the ground seeds and the spice mixture and nuts, raisins and toasted bread and tortillas, whirling until smooth and sauce-like, adding stock as needed to keep it thin enough to be smooth.

13. Combine the two mixtures in a saucepan. Add the vinegar and stir in the chocolate. Simmer for about 20 minutes, adding more stock as needed. The final result should be a rich, spicy paste.

14. Season with salt, pepper, cinnamon, and vinegar to taste.

15. To serve, thin the mole paste with warm stock until it reaches the desired consistency. Warm turkey in remaining oil; warm, too, a stack of corn tortillas. Serve the warm turkey blanketed with the mole sauce, sprinkled with remaining sesame seeds and green onions and/or cilantro, accompanied by a stack of warm corn tortillas, cabbage, and sour cream.

NUTRITIONAL INFORMATION

	TOTAL FAT	SAT FAT	CHOL	ENERGY
Total	323g	57g	633mg	5133kcals

VARIATIONS
MOLE TACOS

Prepare tortillas, preferably fresh. Heat 3–4 tbsp. mole dissolved in ⅔–1 cup chicken stock and simmer until thick and sauce-like. Spoon on to tortillas, then top with shredded cabbage, cilantro, chopped onion, and garlic with sour cream or fromage frais.

ENCHILADAS DE MOLE ROJO
Recipe on page 38.

BARBECUED DUCK BREASTS WITH MOLE

Serve skinless broiled duck breast, slightly charred on the outside, rare inside with a puddle of warm simmered mole. Sprinkle with toasted sesame seeds, pickled jalapeños, chopped green onions, and offer warm tortillas. For an exotic garnish, strew the duck and mole with unsprayed rose petals.

TIME-SAVING VARIATION

Use chili powder(s), preferably homemade from individual chilis, instead of whole chilis and peanut butter in place of the various nuts. Bread may be omitted, and tortilla chips used in place of fried tortilla strips.

CALDO DEL RES
BEEF STOCK AND MEAT

This makes a light stock, good for soups and casseroles; it yields a pot of tender meats for tacos and so forth.

MAKES 5 PINTS STOCK

2lb. beef chuck, flank steak, or brisket per 5–9 cups of cold water

1–2lb. oxtails

8 cloves garlic, coarsely chopped

2 onions, coarsely chopped

1 bay leaf

1 stalk celery, including leaves

dash of cloves

1tsp. dried thyme

1tsp. dried oregano

salt and pepper

5 pints cold water

2 beef bouillon cubes (optional)

1. Combine the beef, oxtails, garlic, onion, bay leaf, celery, cloves, thyme, oregano, salt, and pepper in a large pot and fill with cold water.

2. Bring to a boil, skimming off all the while the grey scum that forms on the top of the pot.

3. Reduce the heat to a slow simmer, add the bouillon cubes if using, and cook the meat, covered, for 3 hours, or until the meat is very tender and the stock full-flavored.

NUTRITIONAL INFORMATION

	TOTAL FAT	SAT FAT	CHOL	ENERGY
Total	255g	115g	1303mg	5921kcals

VARIATION
BROWN STOCK

Sear the meat in a little oil before simmering it with water and herbs.

ROPA VIEJA

OLD CLOTHES IN TATTERS

The pungent garnish of cilantro is lovely on this rich, meaty dish; for variety, garnish the meat with fresh mint or watercress instead.

SERVES 4

2 onions, chopped

5 cloves garlic, chopped

1–2tbsp. oil, or as needed

1–2lb. flank steak from Caldo de Res (page 23), shredded with two forks or your fingers

5 ripe tomatoes or 1½ cups canned, diced

dash of sugar

salt

⅛–¼tsp. ground cumin

⅛–¼tsp. ground cinnamon

dash of allspice

1–2tsp. mild chili powder

1 marinated chipotle chili, diced, plus 1–2tsp. of the marinade

¼tsp. dried oregano

a few drops of vinegar

3tbsp. chopped fresh cilantro

¼ cabbage, thinly sliced, dressed with 1tsp. each of olive oil and vinegar

1. Fry the onions and garlic in the oil until softened then add the meat and brown for a few minutes.

2. Add the tomatoes, sugar, salt, cumin, cinnamon, allspice, chili powder, chipotle chili and marinade, and oregano. Cook over low to medium heat until the meat is richly browned in a small amount of thick sauce.

3. Serve hot, sprinkled with cilantro and cabbage.

NUTRITIONAL INFORMATION				
	TOTAL FAT	SAT FAT	CHOL	ENERGY
Total	173g	73g	683mg	2824kcals
Per Serving	43g	18g	171mg	706kcals

CARNE MACHACA

SHREDDED BEEF
WITH SEASONING

SERVES 4

1 onion, diced

3 cloves garlic, chopped

1tbsp. vegetable oil

1–2lb. tender simmered beef from Caldo del Res (page 23), shredded with two forks

3 ripe tomatoes, diced

2 large mild green chilis such as poblano or Anaheim, roasted, peeled and diced, or 2 green peppers and 2 medium-sized green chilis such as jalapeño, all roasted, peeled and diced

½tsp. crushed dried oregano

½tsp. ground cumin

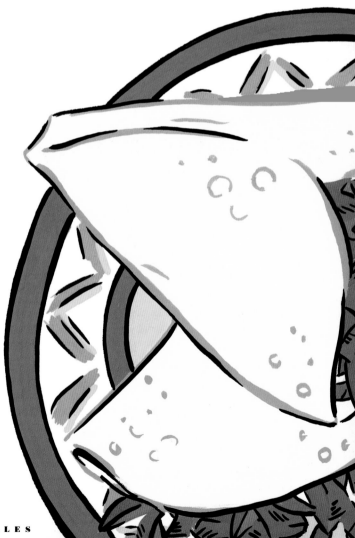

1. Lightly fry the onion and garlic in the oil until softened.

2. Add the meat, tomatoes, chilis, oregano, and cumin and continue to cook for about 15 minutes, adding a little Caldo del Res stock now and again to keep the meat from becoming too dry.

3. Serve as a filling for tacos, etc, or heaped on to a plate surrounded by beans, rice, salsa, and salad.

NUTRITIONAL INFORMATION				
	TOTAL FAT	SAT FAT	CHOL	ENERGY
Total	172g	73g	683mg	2705kcals
Per Serving	43g	18g	171mg	676kcals

COCIDO

SIMMERED DISH OF MEAT, VEGETABLES, AND FRUIT

A cocido is a simmered dinner, much like the puchero of Spain, pot au feu of France, and bollito misto of Italy. From one pot you have a rich stock to eat as a soup course. The second course yields a variety of meats and vegetables: serve on a platter along with boiled potatoes, and several salsas (choose from the Salsa chapter).

Because of its abundance, a cocido is a dish you make in a huge pot: throughout the coming week you will have the basis for many homey, flavorful meals that can be put together almost instantly.

This particular cocido makes a stock that is spicy from chili and chorizo, yet slightly sweet and fragrant from the fruit.

Other vegetables may be added to the pot: part-boiled potatoes or sweet potatoes, ears of corn, strips of sweet red bell pepper, yellow summer squash.

SERVES 6-8

2lb. boneless pork, either in one chunk or bite-sized pieces

2 bay leaves

1 onion, chopped

3 cloves garlic, chopped

2tbsp. chopped fresh cilantro

1 carrot, thinly sliced

2 stalks celery, diced

2 chicken bouillon cubes

½ chorizo (3–4oz.), cut into 2–3 pieces

1 rock cornish game hen or ½ chicken, cut into serving or half-serving pieces

4–5 tomatoes, chopped

½–1 guajillo chili, soaked and puréed, or 1–2tsp. coarsely ground toasted guajillo or other mild chili powder

grated zest of ¼–½ orange

juice of 3 oranges

1 zucchini, cut into bite-sized pieces

¼ cabbage, thinly sliced and blanched

1 apple, cut into bite-sized pieces

10 prunes, pitted

¼tsp. ground cinnamon

dash of dried ginger

salt

1. Combine the pork, bay leaves, onion, garlic, cilantro, carrot, and celery in a large pot and fill with water.

2. Bring to a boil then reduce the heat and simmer over a low heat. Skim the scum that forms when mixture boils first time, but leave any subsequent scum.

3. Add the bouillon cubes and cook for 1 hour or until the meat is becoming tender, then add the chorizo, game hen or chicken, tomatoes, chili, cumin, and orange zest. Continue to cook for another 30 minutes and skim off the fat that forms at the surface.

4. Add the orange juice, zucchini, cabbage, apple, prunes, cinnamon, and ginger and continue to simmer for another 15 minutes or until the zucchini is tender.

5. Season with salt and serve in two courses: with tender boiled noodles or rice for a first course and with boiled potatoes for a second course. Accompany with Salsa de Muchos Chilis y Jitomate (page 18) or other fresh salsa to taste.

NUTRITIONAL INFORMATION				
	TOTAL FAT	SAT FAT	CHOL	ENERGY
Total	112g	39g	990mg	2689kcals
Per Serving (6)	18g	6.5g	165mg	448kcals
Per Serving (8)	14g	5g	124mg	336kcals

MOCHOMOS

SHREDDED PORK
WITH GUACAMOLE

SERVES 4

2lb. very tender cooked pork

vegetable oil

salt and pepper

TO GARNISH

guacamole

shredded lettuce

2tbsp. chopped fresh cilantro

2tbsp. chopped onion

cherry tomatoes or other strong-flavored tomatoes, chopped

fresh salsa

1. Shred the meat into fine strips, then brown in a small amount of oil if needed. Season well with salt and pepper.
2. Serve the hot meat garnished with guacamole, shredded lettuce, cilantro, onion, and tomatoes and offer fresh salsa as desired.

NUTRITIONAL INFORMATION

	TOTAL FAT	SAT FAT	CHOL	ENERGY
Total	91g	23g	760mg	1885kcals
Per Serving	23g	5.5g	190mg	471kcals

PUERCO EN MOLE VERDE
PORK
IN GREEN CHILI SAUCE

Pork in green mole is one of Mexico's great classics (and simple to prepare as well). Pork cooked in stock until just tender is then simmered in tomatillo sauce. The tart tomatillos counteract the richness of the pork.

SERVES 4

2 cloves garlic, chopped

1lb. cooked, drained tomatillos, puréed

3–4 serrano chilis or 2–3 jalapeño chilis, chopped

3tbsp. oil

1 cup pork stock from Caldo de Puerco (page 21)

2lb. pork from Caldo de Puerco

2–3tbsp. mixed chopped fresh herbs: parsley, watercress, cilantro, and purslane, if available

1. In a blender or food processor, purée the garlic with the tomatillos and chilis.
2. Heat the oil in a pan and pour the tomatillo mixture in. Cook over a medium high heat for about 10 minutes or until thickened.
3. Add the stock and meat and continue to simmer for 1–1½ hours or until the meat is tender.
4. Serve sprinkled with chopped fresh herbs.

NUTRITIONAL INFORMATION

	TOTAL FAT	SAT FAT	CHOL	ENERGY
Total	164.5g	52.5g	1380mg	3265kcals
Per Serving	41g	13g	345mg	816kcals

CARNITAS
CRISPY TENDER PORK

SERVES 4

3–4lb. pork, use a cut such as a shoulder that has its bone in place and a bit of fat in the meat

1 onion, chopped

3 cloves garlic, coarsely chopped

1tsp. ground cumin

1tsp. ground coriander

1tsp. dried oregano

2 bay leaves

1–2 chicken bouillon cubes

salt and pepper to taste

1. Prepare pork as in Caldo de Puerco (page 21). As an optional seasoning, add ½ chopped chili chipotle to the simmering stock.
2. Place the meat in a large roasting pan. Season with salt and pepper and bake, uncovered, in a preheated oven at 450°F until sizzling and browned, 20–30 minutes. Pull chunks of meat off the bone and shred with two forks. Discard the fat and serve meat warm, with a selection of salsas. Tortillas, rice, and beans round out the meal authentically.

TAMALES

A good tamale is memorable: tender steamed masa dough, slightly mealy, moist yet never gummy. It should taste of stoneground corn and antiquity.

A tamale may be filled with nearly any sort of savory or sweet filling: meat or poultry in mole; vegetables in pipian; seafood in red chili paste; pineapple and brown sugar; or cheese and green chilis. Alternatively, it may be left unfilled, traditional in many regions as an accompaniment for celebratory feasts.

An unfilled tamale may have bits of vegetables beaten into the masa: kernels of corn are delicious; so, too, are bits of golden squash flowers or enough simmered black beans to stud the dough like little grey-black dots.

Lard is the traditional fat used in making tamales. It needs to be whipped until fluffy and light, then the masa is beaten in, and slowly, very slowly, enough warm stock to make a light dough. I have experimented using both butter and oil as substitutes for lard. The results are not as fine as the lard-based traditional method, but nice enough for me to want to make them again.

TAMALES

SERVES 6

TAMALE DOUGH

about 20 dried corn husks

8oz. masa harina

2tsp. baking powder

1½tsp. salt

⅓ cup vegetable oil

generous 1½ cups lukewarm stock

FILLING

shredded beef or pork seasoned with mole or any sauce of red chilis, Picadillo (page 66), or any chili-seasoned meat, chicken, or fish

1. Place the corn husks in a bowl and pour boiling water over them. Let rest for at least 30 minutes or until the corn husks soften and become pliable. Remove from the water and wipe dry.

2. Combine the masa harina with the baking powder and salt. Stir to mix well, then whisk in the oil, letting the mixture form very light and fluffy grains.

3. Using a wooden spoon, stir in the stock, increasing the amount you add as you stir continuously. When the mixture forms a light dough it is ready.

4. To form the tamales, first lay out a pliable piece of corn husk and spread with masa dough, then lay one on each side and spread those, too, until you have a rectangle that is spread with masa dough, leaving ½ inch or so border around the edges.

5. Place 1–2tbsp. of the filling in the center of each, then fold over the sides, squeezing a bit to seal the masa dough and husks. Fold over the open ends and pile into a steamer. Repeat until the dough or corn husks are used up.

6. Steam over boiling water at a steady bubble for 1 hour. Remove from the steamer.

7. Eat right away, or reheat later by steaming for 30 minutes.

NUTRITIONAL INFORMATION			
	TOTAL FAT	SAT FAT	CHOL	ENERGY
Total	98g	11g	0mg	1729kcals
Per Serving	16.5g	2.0g	0mg	288kcals

GOAT'S CHEESE AND ROASTED GREEN CHILI TAMALES

SERVES 6

1 quantity of tamale dough and corn husks (page 28)

8oz. mild goat's cheese, such as Montrachet, cut into small chunks

2–3 roasted, peeled poblano chilis, lightly marinated in a little garlic, olive oil, and lemon and cut into thin strips

1–2tbsp. chopped fresh cilantro

1. Spread out the dough as directed in the recipe on page 28 then place on it 1tbsp. of goat's cheese, strips of chili and a sprinkling of fresh cilantro.

2. Close up and steam as on page 28. Serve hot.

NUTRITIONAL INFORMATION				
	TOTAL FAT	SAT FAT	CHOL	ENERGY
Total	143g	37.5g	0mg	2274kcals
Per Serving	24g	6.25g	0mg	379kcals

TAMALES DE PESCADO CON ENSALADA
FISH TAMALES
WITH WATERCRESS SALAD

Fish tamales are popular throughout Mexico. Instead of sea bass, shrimp may be used.

SERVES 6

1 quantity tamale dough (page 28), using fish stock instead of chicken stock

20 corn husks as in above recipe or several banana leaves, cut into 12 × 12inch pieces

FILLING

1lb. sea bass fillets or other white-fleshed fish, cut into bite-sized pieces

Red Chili-Citrus Paste (page 18)

1tbsp. chopped fresh cilantro

watercress salad, dressed in olive oil and vinegar

1. Prepare the masa dough for tamales. Set aside.

2. Soak the corn husks (see page 28). Set aside to soften.

3. Combine the fish with the chili paste and cilantro.

4. Form the tamales as on page 28, using the fish filling. (If using banana leaves, make them pliable by heating over the flame gently for a moment or so, then filling and folding into an envelope shape.) Place the parcels in a steamer and cook over medium-high heat for about 40 minutes, adding more water to the steamer if needed to keep them from scorching.

5. Serve hot or leave to cool and heat as desired. Serve with watercress salad.

NUTRITIONAL INFORMATION

	TOTAL FAT	SAT FAT	CHOL	ENERGY
Total	102g	11.5g	230mg	2129kcals
Per Serving	17g	2.0g	38mg	355kcals

VARIATION

For a lighter version of the fish tamale, omit the dough entirely and simply wrap the chili-seasoned fish chunks in the soaked corn husks or warmed banana leaves. Dab a bit of masa harina paste on the soaked corn husks to help them stick together, then steam. Serve with wedges of lime and fresh cilantro.

POSOLE

Posole (also spelled pozole) was eaten in pre-Columbian Mexico. It is no more than kernels of a specific type of corn, cooked in a solution of slaked lime to soften and swell them.

The process pops off their skins, giving the plump corn a unique, earthy flavor and mealy yet chewy consistency. (This is the same corn preparation mashed into a dough and used for tortillas, tamales, and grits.)

Posole is the quintessential Mexican comfort food, spooned up at a Mexican street-stall, a family celebration dinner, or a restaurant (many specialize in posole one day a week). Few other things in life put the world as right as does a bowl of posole.

Anything can be cooked into broth for posole. A large amount of sweet simmered garlic is traditional. So is half a pig's head (though authentic and delicious, it is a bit grisly – spareribs or similar cuts are excellent in its place). Other meats or poultry may be used instead of pork: beef, turkey, lamb, even duck.

SERVES 10-12

1–2lb. dried hominy, or several large cans canned hominy (preferably a combination of white and yellow)

1lb. lean stewing pork or beef

2–3lb. fattier pork meat such as spareribs (or beef, or lamb)

1lb. smoked pork shanks or hocks (optional)

2 beef bouillon cubes

2 chicken bouillon cubes

2 heads of garlic, unpeeled and unseparated, each cut into halves crosswise

2–3 onions, chopped

3 bay leaves

2¼–3lb. chicken

CONDIMENTS

1 onion, chopped

small bowl of fresh oregano leaves, for crumbling

1 cabbage, thinly sliced

1 bunch radishes, cut into julienne strips

2–3 limes, cut into wedges

1 bunch fresh cilantro, chopped

fresh jalapeño peppers, chopped

1. If using dried hominy, soak in water to cover for 8 hours or overnight. Drain.

2. Place the soaked hominy in a large pot with water to cover and simmer for 2–3 hours or until tender. Taste as you go since some hominy cooks quicker than others. If using canned hominy, simply open the cans and drain.

3. Combine the meats, bouillon cubes, garlic, onions, bay leaves, and water to fill the pot.

4. Bring to a boil, reduce the heat to a low simmer, and spoon off any scum that forms at first on the surface. (After that, ignore any more scum – it will cook back into the stock).

5. Cook over a low heat for about 2 hours, then add the chicken. Continue to simmer for another 1½–2½ hours or until the meats are very tender, the chicken tender but not falling apart, and the broth very flavorful.

6. About 30 mins before the broth is ready, add the hominy.

7. Serve the posole in bowls: a few big spoonfuls of hominy, the rich broth, a chunk or two of the various meats and an array of condiments for each eater to add to his or her whim.

NUTRITIONAL INFORMATION				
	TOTAL FAT	SAT FAT	CHOL	ENERGY
Total	271g	130g	2235mg	6979kcals
Per Serving (10)	27g	13g	224mg	698kcals
Per Serving (12)	23g	11g	186mg	582kcals

POSOLE DE HONGOS

WILD MUSHROOM POSOLE

Unlike other posoles, this one is best when subtly spiced since the pairing of forest-scented mushrooms and earthy hominy is lovely. A tiny drop of your favorite fresh salsa is plenty. If using dried mushrooms, break them into small pieces when you combine them with the hot stock. Mushrooms with tough stems such as shiitakes should have their stems removed first and discarded.

SERVES 4 – 6

8oz. fresh flavorful mushrooms such as shiitake, porcini (cèpes), chanterelle or trompets de morte or a combination of dried ones combined with fresh cultivated ones (try 15–20 dried shiitakes plus ½oz. dried porcini and 1 cup fresh cultivated ones)

12–16oz. cooked, drained hominy (page 31)

a few drops to a few tbsp. of your favorite salsa (depending on its strength)

salt and pepper

slices of Monterey Jack cheese (optional)

1. If using fresh mushrooms, combine with hot stock and bring to a boil. If using dried and cultivated combined, pour the hot stock over the dried and fresh mushrooms, cover and leave for 30 minutes.

2. Add the hominy and salsa. Simmer for another 15–25 minutes or until the flavors are melded.

3. Season with salt and pepper and serve right away, either as it is or ladled over a slab of cheese.

NUTRITIONAL INFORMATION				
	TOTAL FAT	SAT FAT	CHOL	ENERGY
Total	5.5g	0.5g	0mg	2098kcals
Per Serving (4)	1.5g	0.1g	0mg	524kcals
Per Serving (6)	1.0g	0.1g	0mg	350kcals

CHAPTER THREE

CASSEROLES, EGG DISHES, AND VEGETARIAN MEALS

★ ★ ★ ★ ★

CAZUELAS

CASSEROLE DISHES

Everywhere you go in Mexico you see them: gaily painted rustic earthenware casseroles, containing savory mixtures of all sorts of things bubbling away. Stuffed tortillas, tortillas layered with sauces, pasta and rice dishes – all are part of the rich variety of main course on offer. The classic paella, a magnificent casserole of rice and seafood, is included here, and a homey dish of fideos – broth-cooked pasta.

CHILAQUILES CON POLLO

CHICKEN CHILAQUILES

Chilaquiles is a casserole of broken up tortillas – its name, in fact, means broken up old sombreros – layered with spicy sauce, meat or poultry, often with a cheesy topping. Sour cream, fried chorizo or eggs – scrambled or fried – are often part of the dish.

Chilaquiles are often made in marketplace cafés, crisp and firm in the morning when they are put on sale, delectably mushy late in the day as the tortillas begin to dissolve in the sauce. It's hard to know which way they are more delicious.

SERVES 6

12 stale tortillas, cut into strips

vegetable oil

1 small to medium chicken, shredded or pulled apart into small pieces

salt and pepper to taste

Mild Salsa Verde de Tomatillos (page 15)

2 mint leaves

2tbsp. chopped fresh cilantro

5 cloves garlic, chopped

¼tsp. ground cumin

1½ cups sour cream or crème fraîche

12oz. white cheese such as Mozzarella, Manchego or Monterey Jack, coarsely shredded

1–1½ cups Parmesan or similar cheese such as Pecorino Romano, shredded

TO SERVE

3–4tbsp. chopped fresh cilantro

1 onion, diced or sliced

2 hardcooked eggs, sliced

thinly sliced chilis or salsa as desired

1. Toss the tortilla strips lightly with a small amount of oil then arrange on a baking sheet. Bake in a preheated oven at 350°F until they are crisp and golden, about 30 minutes. Check often; when crisp, remove and set aside.

2. Arrange the chicken in a 9 × 13inch or 12 × 12inch baking casserole then sprinkle with salt and pepper and half the salsa verde, a leaf of mint and a sprinkling of cilantro, garlic, and cumin, half the sour cream or crème fraîche, and half the tortilla strips. Top with half the cheese, then repeat until everything is used up, ending with a layer of cheese.

3. Bake, covered, in the oven at 350°F for 35–40 minutes, then uncover and continue baking until the cheese is lightly golden in spots.

4. Serve right away, garnished with cilantro, onion, hardcooked egg and chilis or salsa.

NUTRITIONAL INFORMATION

	TOTAL FAT	SAT FAT	CHOL	ENERGY
Total	270g	139g	1450mg	5351kcals
Per Serving	45g	23g	242mg	892kcals

VEGETARIAN VARIATION

Omit the chicken. Serve with black beans on the side.

YUCATECAN ENCHILADAS OF HARDCOOKED EGG AND PUMPKIN SEEDS

Topped with pickled onions, that quintessential Yucatecan relish, these enchiladas are filled with diced hardcooked eggs and sauced with both a tomato and a ground pumpkin seed sauce.

SERVES 6

15 small or 8 medium tomatoes, lightly charred on an ungreased pan

2 small to medium onions, halved, lightly charred then peeled and chopped

1 onion, raw and chopped

10 cloves garlic, lightly charred in their peel then squeezed out

3 cloves garlic, raw and chopped

⅓ cup olive oil

1½ Scots bonnet or chili habañero, or 3 yellow guero chilis, chopped

salt

1½ cups chicken stock

½ head garlic, unpeeled

1tbsp. chopped fresh cilantro

8oz. pumpkin seeds, shelled but raw

12 tortillas

8–12 hardcooked eggs, chopped

TO SERVE

pickled onions

1. In a blender or food processor, purée the charred tomatoes, charred onions, half the raw onions, the charred garlic, and raw garlic. Heat 1tbsp. of oil in a pan then add the tomato purée and half the chilis and cook until the mixture thickens and the oil separates. Season with salt and thin out with chicken stock until the mixture is a light tomato sauce consistency. Set aside.

2. Combine the remaining onion, remaining chilis, cilantro and unpeeled garlic in a saucepan with the remaining chicken stock. Bring to the boil then reduce the heat and simmer until the garlic is tender.

3. Lightly toast the pumpkin seeds in a heavy skillet carefully so that they do not burn – they will pop and sputter out of the pan. When toasted, place in a blender or food processor and grind until mealy, then add the simmered garlic and onion plus a little of the stock to the pumpkin seeds and purée until a paste forms. Stir in enough stock to thicken.

4. Warm the tortillas in the remaining oil to make them pliable, then dip each into the warm pumpkin-seed sauce. Spoon a bit of chopped egg along the center, then roll up and place in a casserole or baking dish.

5. Cover with foil and keep warm in a preheated oven at 350°F while you heat the tomato and pumpkin-seed sauces, taking care that the pumpkin-seed sauce does not overcook and curdle.

6. Serve the papadzules with pumpkin-seed sauce and tomato sauce spooned over, and pickled onions on the side.

NUTRITIONAL INFORMATION				
	TOTAL FAT	SAT FAT	CHOL	ENERGY
Total	266g	45g	1903mg	4731kcals
Per Serving	44g	7.5g	317mg	788kcals

LAYERED CASSEROLE OF SHARK AND TORTILLAS, CAMPECHE STYLE

Typical of the Yucatan, these tortillas are usually fried until puffed then slit and stuffed. Here I have simplified the process by layering the tortillas with the stuffing.
Most types of shark are marvelous with the beans, tomato sauce, and tortillas; if shark is unavailable, any firm-fleshed fish fillet can be substituted.

SERVES 4

1½lb. shark steaks

2½tsp. fresh oregano, crumbled

2 onions, chopped

6 cloves garlic, whole but unpeeled

2tbsp. orange juice

2tbsp. lime juice

grated zest of ½ orange and ¼ lime

1tsp. sugar

fish bouillon cube or 1 cup clam juice mixed with an equal amount of water (optional)

salt and pepper

¼ cup vegetable oil

½ chili habañero or Scots bonnet or 2 serrano or jalapeño chilis, chopped

2lb. tomatoes, diced

2tbsp. grapefruit juice

1 quantity Frijoles Refritos (page 12), made with black beans and seasoned with chili, heated through and kept warm

12 tortillas

TO GARNISH

2–3tbsp. chopped fresh cilantro

2 fresh serrano or jalapeño chilis, thinly sliced

1. Place the shark with 2tsp. oregano, half the onion and the whole garlic cloves in a saucepan. Add water to cover, as well as the bouillon cube or clam juice, if using. Bring to a boil then reduce the heat and simmer very gently for about 10 minutes. Remove from the heat and let the fish cool in the stock. Season with salt and pepper, then remove the fish from the stock and shred or pull apart into small pieces.

2. To make the sauce, heat 2tbsp. oil in a skillet and fry the remaining onion until softened. Add the chili, tomatoes, and citrus juices and zest. Season with the remaining oregano and thin with a little of the stock from simmering the fish.

3. Warm the tortillas in a small amount of the oil then arrange 4 in a casserole. Spread with warm black beans then top with a layer of fish. Add another tortilla layer and a layer of sauce, then another layer of tortillas, black beans and fish, then a final layer of tortillas and sauce. Cover with foil or a lid and bake for about 10 minutes in a preheated oven at 450°F. Garnish with fresh cilantro and chilis as well as any leftover sauce.

NUTRITIONAL INFORMATION				
	TOTAL FAT	SAT FAT	CHOL	ENERGY
Total	140g	23g	375mg	5574kcals
Per Serving	35g	5.75g	94mg	1394kcals

ENCHILADAS DE ELOTES
CORN ENCHILADAS
WITH TOMATO-RED CHILI SAUCE

Corn kernels mixed with cheese, half puréed and half chunky makes a marvelous filling for enchiladas.

SERVES 4

2¼ cups cooked corn kernels, lightly drained

½ cup cottage or Ricotta cheese

2 cloves garlic, chopped

about ½ fresh green chili such as jalapeño, chopped

salt

dash of sugar

½tsp. ground cumin

2tbsp. chopped fresh cilantro

8oz. sharp white cheese such as fresh Pecorino, Cheddar, or a mixture of Monterey Jack, Asiago, and Parmesan

9 corn tortillas

1–2tbsp. vegetable oil

6oz. tomatoes, fresh or canned, with their juice

⅓ cup vegetable stock

1tbsp. mild chili powder

dash of chipotle chili powder (toasted, ground dried chipotle chili) or drop chipotle marinade or salsa

1. Combine the corn with the cottage or Ricotta cheese, half the garlic, the fresh chili, salt, sugar, cumin, cilantro, half the cheese, and 1 tortilla, thinly sliced or chopped.

2. Whirl half this mixture in a blender or food processor then combine with with the half that has not been puréed.

3. Heat the remaining tortillas in oil to soften, then spoon a few tablespoons of filling on to the edge of each and roll up. Place each rolled tortilla in a baking dish.

4. Combine the remaining garlic with the tomatoes, vegetable stock, chili powder, chipotle powder or marinade if using. Spoon over the sauce. Top with the remaining cheese.

5. Bake in a preheated oven at 400°F oven until heated through and the cheese topping has melted.

NUTRITIONAL INFORMATION				
	TOTAL FAT	SAT FAT	CHOL	ENERGY
Total	111g	59g	266mg	2922kcals
Per Serving	28g	15g	67mg	730 kcals

ENCHILADAS VERDES

GREEN-TOMATO ENCHILADAS

Enchiladas verdes are one of the most irresistible dishes in the Mexican kitchen. Simple to prepare, the tangy tomatillo sauce balances the richness of the cheese and the heartiness of the tortillas.
Simmered chicken, pork, or beef can be used as filling instead of the cheese; in New Mexico these would come with a golden-yolked egg plunked enticingly on top.

SERVES 4

1lb. cooked tomatillos, puréed (or use canned)

2 cloves garlic, chopped

1 onion, chopped

½ jalapeño chili, chopped

1tbsp. chopped fresh cilantro

½ cup chicken or vegetable stock

salt and pepper

⅛tsp. ground cumin

10–12 corn tortillas

vegetable oil

1lb. mild cheese such as Monterey Jack, Gouda, Mozzarella or Cheddar, or a combination, coarsely shredded

sour cream, to garnish

½ onion, chopped, to garnish

fresh salsa of choice, to serve

1. Combine the tomatillos, garlic, onion, jalapeño, and cilantro with the stock in a pan and bring to a boil. Simmer for 15–25 minutes or just long enough to blend the flavors. Season with salt, pepper, and cumin.

2. Warm the tortillas in a lightly oiled heavy-based skillet then dip into the warm tomatillo sauce. Place 1–2tbsp. of shredded cheese along one side and roll up, reserving enough cheese for sprinkling on top of the casserole.

3. Arrange in a baking dish. Sprinkle with cheese and cumin, then bake in a preheated oven at 375°F until the cheese melts.

4. Serve immediately, garnished with sour cream and chopped onion. Offer salsa of choice on the side.

NUTRITIONAL INFORMATION

	TOTAL FAT	SAT FAT	CHOL	ENERGY
Total	171g	103g	530mg	3406kcals
Per Serving	42g	26g	133mg	851kcals

VARIATION
PASILLA-PAINTED ENCHILADAS VERDES

Lightly toast 2 pasilla chilis, then pour hot water over them. Leave to soak until they rehydrate; to hurry the process simmer for about 20 minutes. When cool enough to handle, remove the stems, open the chilis up and, using a sharp paring knife, remove the seeds and inner veins. Carefully scrape the flesh from the papery skin. Take this rich concentrated pasilla flesh and purée it with ¼ cup chicken or vegetable stock. Drizzle on to the enchiladas before you sprinkle with cheese, then bake.

ENCHILADAS DE MOLE ROJO

ENCHILADAS IN RED MOLE

This casserole of tortillas dipped in a rich chili, nut, and seed sauce and topped with garbanzo beans and cheese is a delicious mix of complex earthy flavors.

This is an elaboration of a similar enchilada I ate on a bus ride through the mountains of Mexico's interior. At various points in the seemingly endless and sometimes perilous drive our bus stopped in little villages for rest and food. Women came out bearing earthenware casseroles filled with a wide variety of dishes prepared for us, all for but a few pesos.

SERVES 4

- 2 tbsp. toasted sesame seeds
- 2–3 tbsp. roasted peanuts
- 2 tbsp. ancho chili powder
- 1 tbsp. hot paprika or very mild chili powder (or soak 3 ancho chilis then purée with a little of the soaking liquid)
- ⅛–¼ tsp. ground cinnamon
- dash of ground cloves
- ⅛–¼ tsp. dried thyme
- ⅛–¼ tsp. dried oregano
- ⅛–¼ tsp. dried marjoram
- dash of pepper
- 1½ cups water
- salt
- 3 cloves garlic, minced
- 3–4 tbsp. oil
- juice of 1 lime
- 12 corn tortillas
- approx ¾ lb. cooked beef
- 2 cups cooked, drained garbanzo beans

a little chicken or vegetable stock

4oz. fresh white cheese such as Gueso Fresco, fresh Pecorino or a not too salty Feta, lightly crumbled

TO SERVE

1 waxy potato, boiled and cubed

1 carrot, boiled and cubed

1tsp. vinegar

shredded lettuce

1 cup sour cream

2tbsp. chopped fresh cilantro

2 green onions, thinly sliced

jalapeños en escabeche

1. In a spice or coffee grinder, grind the sesame seeds and peanuts to a fine meal.

2. Place it with the chili powder and paprika (or puréed chilis), cinnamon, cloves, thyme, oregano, marjoram, pepper, water, salt, and garlic in a blender or food processor and whirl to make a smooth sauce.

3. Heat 2–3tbsp. oil in a skillet then pour in the sauce. Cook, scraping up the bottom, for about 10 minutes or until the sauce becomes rich in flavor and darkened in color. Stir in the lime juice and set aside.

4. Heat the tortillas in an oiled pan until softened, then spread each with some of the red chili and seed sauce. Fill with a few spoonfuls of meat then roll up. Arrange each rolled tortilla in a casserole. When all the tortillas have been filled, sprinkle with garbanzo beans and the remaining sauce.

5. Spoon over a little chicken or vegetable stock then sprinkle with cheese. Place in a preheated oven at 400°F and heat through until the enchiladas are hot and the cheese is melted.

6. Toss the potato and carrot with vinegar.

7. Serve garnished with potato and carrot, lettuce, sour cream, cilantro, green onions, and jalapeños en escabeche.

NUTRITIONAL INFORMATION				
	TOTAL FAT	SAT FAT	CHOL	ENERGY
Total	151g	58g	238mg	3525kcals
Per Serving	38g	14g	59mg	881kcals

LOWER FAT VARIATION

Substitute fromage frais for sour cream and use a low-fat cheese.

SOPA SECA DE FIDEOS

DRY SOUP OF PASTA
IN MILD CHILI SAUCE WITH CHEESE

Sopa seca translates literally as "dry soup", a name given to pasta and rice dishes cooked in broth to a thick, casserole-like consistency. It is a consummate comfort food, as good eaten with a spoon alone late at night as it is in a more sociable setting, sitting around the table.

SERVES 4

12oz. very thin pasta such as capellini, nidi, or coiled fideo

2–3 bay leaves

2–3 Mexican chorizo sausages, about 3oz. each, cut into bite-sized pieces (or spicy, unsmoked Spanish chorizo)

1 onion, chopped

1 green pepper or mild green chili such as Anaheim or poblano, thinly sliced

4–5 cloves garlic, chopped

1½ cups tomato sauce, chopped tomatoes or passata

1½ cups hot but not boiling chicken, meat, or vegetable stock

crumbled dry oregano to taste

3 cups coarsely shredded sharp cheese or combination creamy mild cheese and sharp cheese

2tbsp. chopped fresh cilantro

1. Boil the pasta with the bay leaves until the pasta is just al dente. Drain and discard bay leaves.

2. Fry the chorizo; when it begins to brown add the onion and pepper or chili and continue to cook until they have softened. Add the garlic, tomato sauce, chopped tomatoes or passata, stock, and oregano.

3. Toss the drained pasta with the sauce mixture then place in a baking dish. Cover with grated cheese.

4. Bake in a preheated oven at 400°F until the top is bubbling and lightly browned and the dish is heated well through. Serve immediately, with fresh cilantro.

NUTRITIONAL INFORMATION				
	TOTAL FAT	SAT FAT	CHOL	ENERGY
Total	194g	106g	482mg	3800kcals
Per Serving	48.5g	26.5g	121mg	950kcals

PAELLA

Sunday lunch in the Colonial regions and restaurants of Mexico is time for paella. And what a paella you will find! Rich with a sea-full of creatures, spicy and redolent of garlic, scented with chorizo. Unlike paella in Spain and the Languedoc, paella in Mexico is at its best when accompanied by a bowl of fresh spicy salsa.

Your lunch might begin with a crisp spicy ceviche of whatever is freshest from the sea: tangy with lemon and cooked by the citrus juice, not heat. Warm tortillas accompany the paella, with crisp cooling beer to drink, and afterwards perhaps a dessert of lush tropical fruits or a bowl of comforting eggy crème caramel, perhaps scented with coffee.

SERVES 6-8

1tsp. dried oregano	scant 1 cup tomato passata or 8oz. fresh or canned tomatoes, chopped
5 cloves garlic, chopped	4¼ cups hot chicken stock
1tsp. vinegar	2 large dashes saffron, lightly toasted in an ungreased pan, then crushed in mortar and pestle
2tbsp. olive oil	
1tsp. salt	
1 chicken or rabbit, cut into serving pieces	8oz. squid, cleaned and cut into rings and tentacles
2 chorizos, skinned and chopped	1 cup shrimp in their shells
1 onion, chopped	1½ cups peas, blanched or young green beans, topped and tailed and cut into bite-sized lengths
1 red bell pepper, diced	
1 green bell pepper, diced	
1tsp. ground coriander	6oz. marinated artichoke hearts (optional)
1lb. long-grain easy-cook rice	1lb. clams or mussels

1. Toss the oregano, garlic, vinegar, olive oil, and salt with the chicken or rabbit. Let marinate for at least 30 minutes, preferably overnight.

2. Remove from the marinade. Save any marinade to add when cooking the rice.

3. Fry the chicken with the chorizo in a heavy-based skillet until the chicken is lightly browned and cooked about halfway through and the chorizo has broken into bits. Do not let the chorizo burn; remove it from the pan if it cooks before the chicken.

4. Remove the chicken and chorizo from the pan, leaving behind the savory flavored oil from the cooking. In this cook the onion and peppers, letting them fry lightly until softened. Stir in the cilantro and cook for a few moments longer.

5. Stir in the rice, and cook lightly in the onion-pepper mixture then add the tomatoes and stir in the hot stock. Return the chicken, the chorizo, and any juices that have accumulated, as well as any marinade left over to the pan with the rice and stock. Add the saffron. Cover and cook for about 10 minutes or until the rice is half cooked.

6. Fold in the squid, shrimp, peas or beans, and marinated artichoke hearts, if using, then top the casserole with the clams or mussels. Cover and bake in a preheated oven at 450°F for about 10 minutes longer or until the clams or mussels pop open. Serve immediately.

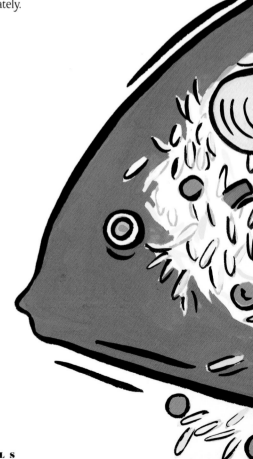

NUTRITIONAL INFORMATION				
	TOTAL FAT	SAT FAT	CHOL	ENERGY
Total	126g	37g	1600mg	4672kcals
Serving (6)	21g	6g	267mg	779kcals
Serving (8)	16g	4.5g	200mg	584kcals

HUEVOS

EGG DISHES

Mexican cuisine is rich in egg dishes – in fact, my favorite dish, although too simple to require a recipe, is a mound of steamed rice topped with 2 poached eggs, lots of sparklingly fresh tomato-green chili salsa and a sprinkling of cilantro.

HUEVOS CON TOTOPOS (MIGAS)

EGGS SCRAMBLED

WITH TOMATOES, CHILIS, AND TORTILLAS

Scrambled with tomatoes, chilis, garlic, and spices, with a handful of crisp tortilla chips stirred in, eggs make a marvelous supper or brunch dish.

SERVES 4

8–10 corn tortillas, cut into ½inch strips (or several large handfuls not too salty or oily tortilla chips)

½ cup vegetable oil

6 cloves garlic, chopped

1 green bell pepper, diced

½ jalapeño or other green chili, thinly sliced or chopped

3 tbsp. butter

1½tsp. ground cumin

5 ripe tomatoes, coarsely chopped

8 eggs, lightly beaten

TO GARNISH

3tbsp. chopped fresh cilantro

3–4 green onions, thinly sliced

1. Fry the tortilla strips in the oil until golden but not dark brown; remove from the oil and drain on paper towels. (If using tortilla chips simply break up into bite-sized pieces.)

2. Fry the garlic, green pepper, and chili in a third of the butter for just 1 minute, then add the cumin and tomatoes and cook over medium heat for 3–4 minutes until the tomatoes are no longer runny. Remove from the pan and set aside.

3. Over low heat, melt the remaining butter in a pan. Pour in the beaten eggs. Cook over low heat, stirring until the eggs begin to set.

4. Add the reserved chili-tomato mixture and tortilla strips and continue cooking, stirring once or twice, until the eggs are the consistency you wish. The tortilla strips should be pliable and chewy, neither crisp nor soggy.

5. Serve immediately, topped with cilantro and green onions.

NUTRITIONAL INFORMATION				
	TOTAL FAT	SAT FAT	CHOL	ENERGY
Total	222g	55g	2007mg	3590kcals
Per Serving	55.5g	13.5g	502mg	897kcals

LOWER FAT VARIATION

Prepare the tortillas as for Fat-Free Totopos (page 11) and omit the oil for frying.

HUEVOS A LA MEXICANA

MEXICAN EGGS

This simple dish consists of egg-topped tortillas, covered with a layer of tangy cheese, studded with chilis and tomatoes and seasoned with garlic. Serve with tender beans, either pinto or black, and rice tinted golden with saffron. Serve your favorite fresh salsa on the side, along with a salad of avocado, roasted red pepper, sliced orange, and red onion.

SERVES 4

drizzle of butter or olive oil

4 corn tortillas

2 cloves garlic, chopped

1–2 green chilis, chopped

3–4 ripe tomatoes, diced

4 eggs, broken into saucers, yolks whole and intact

½tsp. ground cumin or cumin seeds

1½ cups shredded or crumbled cheese such as Pecorino or a mixture of Monterey Jack and Feta

TO GARNISH

2tbsp. chopped onion

2tbsp. chopped fresh cilantro

1. Use a pan that is big enough to take all the tortillas or use two pans. Heat a small amount of butter or oil in the pan(s) and add the tortillas. Scatter the tops of the tortillas with the garlic, green chili, and tomatoes then carefully pour an egg on to each tortilla. Sprinkle with cumin and cheese, cover, and cook over medium low heat until the whites of the egg have firmed and the cheese melted, though the yolks should remain soft.

2. Scatter with onion and cilantro and serve immediately.

NUTRITIONAL INFORMATION				
	TOTAL FAT	SAT FAT	CHOL	ENERGY
Total	65g	31g	1074mg	1401kcals
Per Serving	16g	8g	269mg	350kcals

HUEVOS MOTULENOS
TOMATO-CHILI EGGS

In the Yucatan this classic dish would come sandwiched between two crisp tortillas, but I find that with tortillas on the bottom only, the dish is more visually appealing.

SERVES 4

1¾ cups fresh or canned tomatoes, chopped

1 onion, chopped

3 cloves garlic, minced

1–2 fresh chilis, chopped

salt and pepper

large dash of ground cumin

3tbsp. olive oil

1 plantain, peeled and diced

1 tbsp. butter

4 tostadas (page 11)

Frijoles Refritos (page 12), seasoned with cumin

4 or 8 poached or fried eggs, warm

1 red pepper or fresh large red mild chili such as Anaheim or poblano, roasted, seeded, stemmed and peeled, then cut into strips

3–4tbsp. cooked green peas, warm

3tbsp. diced smoked ham

2tbsp. chopped fresh cilantro

¾ cup flavorful white cheese such as Feta or mild white such as Monterey Jack, diced

1. In a blender or food processor, purée tomatoes with the onion, garlic, chilis, salt and pepper, and cumin.

2. Heat the oil in a skillet then ladle in a little of this sauce and cook until the sauce reduces in volume and becomes almost paste-like. Ladle in some more sauce and repeat. Finally, pour in the remaining sauce and simmer together for 5–10 minutes. Keep warm.

3. Lightly brown the plantain in butter. Set aside and keep warm.

4. Spread the tostadas with warm Frijoles Negros Refritos, then top each with 1 or 2 poached or fried egg(s).

5. Spoon the warm tomato sauce around and/or over the egg, then sprinkle with the diced plantains, roasted peppers or chilis, peas, ham, cilantro, and cheese.

NUTRITIONAL INFORMATION				
	TOTAL FAT	SAT FAT	CHOL	ENERGY
Total	157g	45.5g	1045mg	4494kcals
Per Serving	39g	11.3g	261mg	1123kcals

HUEVOS OAXAQUENA
OAXACA EGGS

Cooking eggs in a flat omelet, then cutting them into strips makes an intriguingly different egg dish .

SERVES 4

2lb. tomatoes

dash of sugar

6 small to medium-sized onions, peeled and halved

10 cloves garlic, whole and unpeeled

2–3 Anaheim or poblano chilis, roasted, peeled and sliced

3 fresh green chilis such as serranos, thinly sliced

⅓ cup oil

salt and pepper

dash of cumin

dash of dried oregano

dash of sugar

8 eggs, lightly beaten

TO GARNISH

2tbsp. chopped fresh cilantro

a little chopped fresh chili (optional)

1. In an ungreased heavy-based pan, lightly char the tomatoes, turning once or twice. Allow to cool.

2. Cut up the tomatoes and place in a blender or food processor with their skins. Lightly char the onions and garlic. Cut up the onions and add to the blender or food processor, then squeeze the garlic cloves out of their skins and add with the chilis. Whirl until a smooth purée is formed.

3. Heat 2tbsp. oil in a skillet then ladle in the sauce. Cook over high heat until it thickens and condenses.

4. Season to taste with salt and pepper, cumin, oregano, and sugar to balance the acid-sweetness. Set aside.

5. Make flat omelets, like thin pancakes, in the remaining oil, cooking about 2 eggs at a time and turning them over. Stack on a plate, and slice into noodle-like ribbons.

6. Heat the omelet strips in the sauce until warmed through, then garnish with cilantro and a little fresh chili.

NUTRITIONAL INFORMATION				
	TOTAL FAT	SAT FAT	CHOL	ENERGY
Total	145g	25g	1903mg	1811kcals
Per Serving	36g	6.25g	476mg	453kcals

CASSEROLES, EGG DISHES, AND VEGETARIAN MEALS

PATATAS CON CHIPOTLE CREMA Y QUESO DE CABRITA

POTATOES

WITH GOAT'S CHEESE-CHIPOTLE CREAM

This makes a luscious casserole of potatoes baked with tangy goat's cheese and piquant chipotle, rich with cream and melted cheese. Serve with a crisp salad of purslane, chervil, watercress, and other interesting greens, lightly dressed with olive oil and vinegar.

SERVES 4

3lb. baking potatoes, peeled and cut into chunks

salt and pepper

scant 1 cup crème fraîche

½ cup vegetarian stock

4 cloves garlic, chopped

1–2tsp. marinade from chipotles en adobo, or ½ chopped chipotle or mild chili powder to taste

1 log (8oz.) goat's cheese, sliced

1½ cups melting white cheese such as Queso Anejo, medium Asiago, Monterey Jack, Mozzarella, shredded

½–¾ cup Parmesan or Pecorino, shredded

1. Cook the potatoes in rapidly boiling water until half done. Drain and sprinkle with salt and pepper.

2. Combine the crème fraîche with the stock, half the garlic, and the chipotle marinade, chipotle or chili powder.

3. Arrange half the potatoes in a baking casserole then pour half the crème fraîche sauce over the potatoes. Add a layer of goat's cheese, then finish with the remaining potatoes and sauce.

4. Sprinkle with shredded white cheese then with shredded Parmesan or Pecorino.

5. Bake in a preheated oven at 350–375°F until the potatoes are creamy inside and the cheese topping is lightly golden and crisped in places on top. Serve immediately, sprinkled with the remaining garlic.

NUTRITIONAL INFORMATION				
	TOTAL FAT	SAT FAT	CHOL	ENERGY
Total	140g	86g	294mg	3194kcals
Per Serving	35g	21.5g	73mg	798kcals

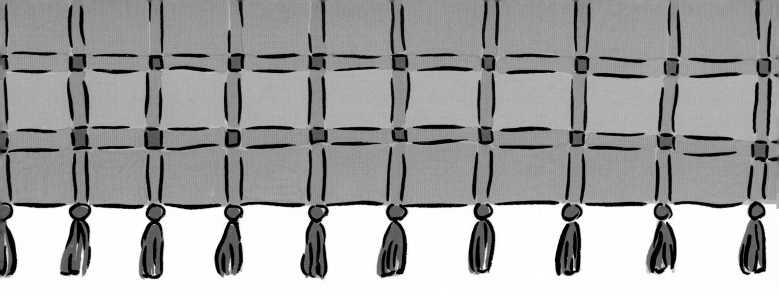

CHAPTER FOUR

BARBECUED
AND BROILED FOODS

★ ★ ★ ★ ★

A LA PARILLA

BARBECUED AND BROILED FOODS

The scent of smoke permeates the air throughout Mexico. In the markets, braziers are set up for impromptu tacos al carbon. In the countryside, a fiesta means a great pit will be dug for a barbacoa, and in restaurants wood-fired grills flavor a wide variety of foods from the land and sea.

CARNE ASADO CON PLATANOS Y SALSA

GRILLED RARE STEAK AND PLANTAINS

WITH CHIPOTLE-TOMATO SALSA

The roasty, meaty flavor of rare steak cooked over the coals is enhanced by a dab of smoky chipotle salsa. Ripe plantains, browned over the coals as well, provide a sweet, starchy sidenote. A bed of greens is refreshing next to the rich meat and plantains; purslane especially is *muy Mexicana*, though usually simmered in a stew rather than served raw. Purslane is seldom sold in grocery stores; the best place to find it is between the plants in your garden. It is a creeping, flat-lying plant that has slightly rounded, almost succulent little leaves. It is unusual and delicious, and recent reports suggest it may be a good source of omega-3 fatty acids. Serve with a mound of rice and black beans, and a bowl of the fiery salsa.

SERVES 4

4 tender steaks such as filet, about 6oz. each

3 cloves garlic, chopped

salt and pepper

1tbsp. olive oil

2 ripe plantains, peeled and cut into halves lengthwise

dash of ground cinnamon

few drops of chipotle marinade or ¼–½ chipotle chili en adobo, chopped

1¾ cups fresh or canned tomatoes, chopped

½ onion, chopped

dash of ground cumin

dash of dried oregano

TO GARNISH

wedges of lime

handful of greens such as watercress, purslane, rocket, or cilantro

1. Rub the meat with about 1 clove of chopped garlic, then sprinkle with salt and pepper. Rub with olive oil and set aside.

2. Sprinkle the plantains with cinnamon and set aside.

3. To make the salsa, combine the chipotle marinade or chopped chipotle with the tomatoes, onion, and remaining garlic; season with cinnamon, cumin, the oregano, and salt and pepper.

4. Cook the steaks over hot coals until lightly charred on the outside, rare within. Depending on the thickness, they should take only about 3–4 minutes on each side.

5. Add the plantains to the grill and cook until lightly browned in spots, about 3 minutes on each side.

6. Serve the steak and plantains garnished with lime wedges, a handful of greens, and chipotle salsa.

NUTRITIONAL INFORMATION				
	TOTAL FAT	SAT FAT	CHOL	ENERGY
Total	45g	15g	413mg	1512 kcals
Per Serving	11g	4g	103mg	378kcals

YUCATECAN STEAK

Barbecuing a handful of green onions alongside whatever else is on the grill is *muy Mexicana*. Cut the onions on the diagonal as otherwise the long strands can stick in the throat.

SERVES 4

4 thin steaks, beef, pork, or venison

3 cloves garlic, chopped

2tbsp. tequila

2tbsp. mild red chili powder

2tbsp. chopped fresh cilantro

juice of ½ orange

juice of 2 or more limes

6–10 green onions, trimmed

6tbsp. olive oil

½ onion, grated

salt

½ white or green cabbage, thinly sliced

dash of dried oregano

½ green chili, thinly sliced

TO SERVE

1 recipe batch of black beans (page 12), refried or simmered with chilis

corn tortillas

salsa of choice

wedges of lime and orange

1. Combine the steaks with the garlic, tequila, chili powder, cilantro, orange juice, 1tbsp. lime juice, green onions, half the olive oil, grated onion, and salt to taste. Let marinate for about 30 minutes.

2. Combine the cabbage with the oregano, green chili, remaining olive oil and lime juice, and salt to taste. (This cabbage relish is even better prepared a day ahead.)

3. Grill the steaks and green onions over hot coals quickly until they are just cooked. Since they are thin, they need only cook a few minutes on each side.

4. Slice the green onions into more easily chewable slices and serve alongside the steaks. Accompany with black beans, corn tortillas, salsa, and wedges of lime and orange.

NUTRITIONAL INFORMATION				
	TOTAL FAT	SAT FAT	CHOL	ENERGY
Total	87g	17.5g	236mg	1348kcals
Per Serving	22g	4.5g	59mg	337kcals

POLLO ROJO CON SALSA DE AGUACATE

RED CHILI-MARINATED CHICKEN BREASTS
WITH AVOCADO SAUCE

Sauces of mashed avocado are frequently spooned up with grilled foods. Their bland flavor balances the spicy scent of the barbecue and the piquant jolt of chili.

SERVES 4

4 boneless half chicken breasts, 7–8oz. each, skin removed

3tbsp. Recado Rojo (page 19) (or mix a good chili powder with chopped garlic, orange juice and zest, plus a dash of ground cumin)

2tbsp. olive oil

juice of 1 lime

2tbsp. chopped fresh cilantro

2 ripe avocados, peeled and lightly mashed

¼ onion, chopped

1. Combine the chicken breasts with 2tbsp. Recado Rojo, the olive oil, half the lime juice, and half the cilantro. Let marinate for at least 30 minutes.

2. To make the sauce, combine the remaining lime juice and coriander with the avocados and remaining Recado Rojo. Season with salt to taste and set aside, covered.

3. Grill the chicken breasts, about 3 minutes per side. Do not overcook.

4. Serve the chicken breasts hot from the barbecue, sprinkled with onion and napped with the spicy avocado sauce.

NUTRITIONAL INFORMATION				
	TOTAL FAT	SAT FAT	CHOL	ENERGY
Total	85g	19g	344mg	1520kcals
Per Serving	21g	4.75g	86mg	380kcals

VARIATION
GRILLED STEAK WITH SALSA DE AGUACATE

In place of chicken breasts, grill tender steaks, rubbed with the same spicy mixture. Cook until rare, only a few minutes on each side.

POLLO ROJO A LA PARILLA

BARBECUED CHICKEN
MARINATED IN ACHIOTE
AND MUSTARD

Achiote seeds, ground into a bright orange powder, have a slightly tangy, slightly saffron scent. They color everything they touch an indelible yellow hue. This is a delicious grilled chicken dish that I tasted in Mexico City.

SERVES 4

1 chicken, 2–3lb. halved or quartered

2tbsp. achiote seeds, ground or puréed

8 cloves garlic, thinly sliced

1 onion, finely chopped, or 5–8 shallots, chopped

1tbsp. sweet paprika

2tbsp. mild chili powder

5tbsp. mild brown flavorful mustard, preferably wholeseed

3tbsp. Dijon-style mustard

3tbsp. olive oil

2tbsp. lemon juice

3tbsp. crème fraîche or sour cream

salt and pepper

1. Combine the chicken with the ground or puréed garlic, onion or shallots, paprika, chili powder, half the mild mustard, the Dijon mustard, olive oil, and lemon juice.

2. Let marinate in the refrigerator, at least overnight and up to 2 days.

3. Cook over medium-hot coals, putting the leg quarters on the grill for 15 minutes (chicken halves take longer, around 20 minutes), then adding the breast quarters and cooking for a further 15 minutes. The chicken is done when the juices run clear when the flesh is pierced.

4. Meanwhile, combine the reserved mustard with the crème fraîche or sour cream.

5. Spread the mustard-crème fraîche mixture over the hot chicken, then sprinkle with salt and pepper. Serve immediately.

NUTRITIONAL INFORMATION				
	TOTAL FAT	SAT FAT	CHOL	ENERGY
Total	90g	24g	657mg	1697kcals
Per Serving	22.5g	6g	164mg	424kcals

BARBECUED AND BROILED FOODS

PESCADO A LA PARILLA

BACON-WRAPPED TROUT

WITH RED CHILI ESSENCE

This is a modern adaptation of the escabeche, that is, lightly pickled, sauce: here, reduced stock is seasoned with vinegar, then poured over a hot grilled fish.

SERVES 4

1 onion, chopped

3 cloves garlic, chopped

2 tbsp. olive oil

2 ripe tomatoes, chopped

1–3 tbsp. mild chili powder

¼ tsp. ground cumin

1½ cups chicken stock

¾ cup dry white wine

2 tbsp. vinegar

4 small to medium-sized trout, cleaned (leave head or remove, as desired)

salt and pepper

4–8 slices smoked bacon, derinded

fresh cilantro leaves, to garnish

1. Fry the onion and garlic in olive oil until softened; do not allow to brown. Add the tomatoes, then stir in the chili powder and cumin and cook for a few moments.

2. Pour in the stock and wine; boil until it reduces in volume to about ¾ cup then add the vinegar. Simmer for another 5 minutes, or until it tastes tangy and flavorful, then remove from the heat.

3. Sprinkle each trout with salt and pepper then wrap with bacon, using 1 or 2 slices per trout, as needed.

4. Grill over hot coals, about 5 minutes per side, or until the fish feels done when gently pressed with the finger.

5. Serve each portion of trout in a bowl with a few spoonfuls of the chili essence poured over. Garnish with cilantro.

NUTRITIONAL INFORMATION				
	TOTAL FAT	SAT FAT	CHOL	ENERGY
Total	61g	12g	426mg	1306kcals
Per Serving	15g	3g	107mg	326kcals

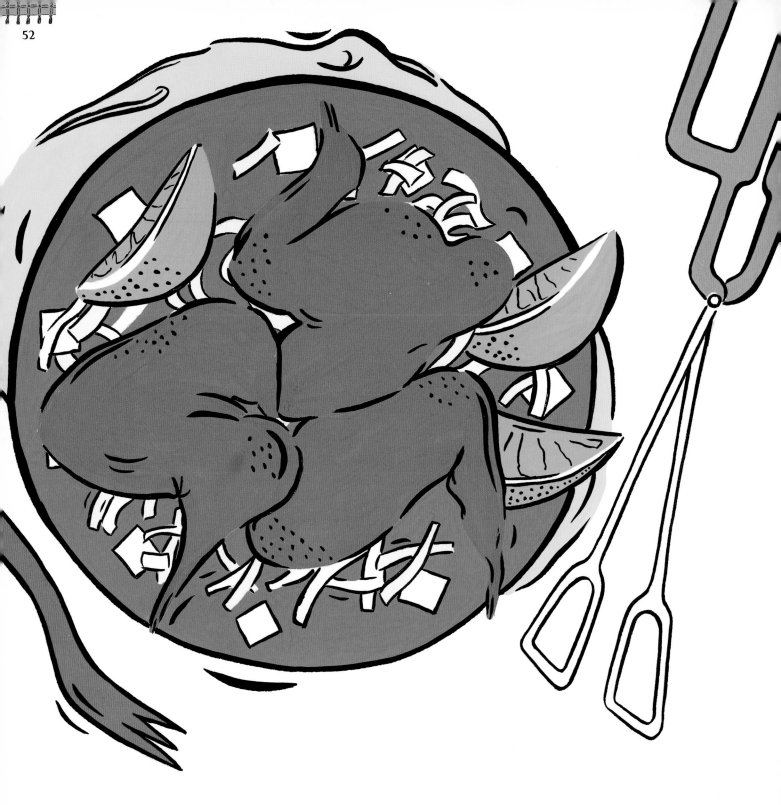

POLLO CON CHILE Y TEQUILA

CHILI-TEQUILA-MARINATED CRISP CHICKEN WINGS

Chili spices season the chicken wings while tequila and citrus juice tenderize them. These are delicious served on their own or with other barbecued foods such as seafood, sausages, and so forth, all accompanied by steamed rice and black beans, and plantains cooked on the grill.

SERVES 4

2–3lb. chicken wings	2tbsp. vegetable oil
5 cloves garlic, chopped	1tsp. sugar
juice of 2 limes	¼tsp. ground allspice
juice of 1 orange	dash of ground cinnamon
2tbsp. tequila	dash of ground cumin
salt and pepper	dash of dried oregano, crumbled
1tbsp. mild chili powder	
2tsp. chipotle marinade or 3 dried chipotle chilis, rehydrated and puréed	

1. Combine the chicken wings with all the other ingredients and let marinate for at least 3 hours, preferably overnight.

2. Cook over hot coals for approximately 15–25 minutes, until the wings are crisply browned, and serve immediately.

NUTRITIONAL INFORMATION				
	TOTAL FAT	SAT FAT	CHOL	ENERGY
Total	56g	13g	475mg	1260 kcals
Per Serving	14g	3g	119mg	315kcals

POLLITO CON SALSA CREMA, PIMIENTO ROJO, Y CHILI CHIPOTLE

GREEN-HERBED GAME HENS

WITH ROASTED RED PEPPER-CHIPOTLE CREAM

This tender poussin dish is both elegant and rustic, and is marvelous accompanied by Mexican rice cooked with corn and a sprinkling of fresh marjoram.

SERVES 4

10 cloves garlic, chopped	salt and pepper
juice of 1 lime	1½ cups crème fraîche or sour cream
3tbsp. olive oil	1 red pepper, roasted, peeled, and diced
2oz. chopped cilantro, plus a little extra for garnish	½–1tsp. marinade from chipotles en adobo
½ green chili, chopped	3–5 green onions, thinly sliced, to garnish (optional)
1tsp. ground cumin	
4 Rock Cornish game hens, spatchcocked	

1. In a blender or food processor, combine 9 cloves garlic with the lime juice, olive oil, cilantro, green chili, and half the cumin. Whirl until it forms a paste.

2. Sprinkle the hens with salt and pepper, then rub well with the green spicy paste. Let marinate for at least 30 minutes at room temperature or up to 48 hours in the refrigerator.

3. Combine the remaining garlic and cumin with the crème fraîche, roasted red pepper, and chipotle marinade.

4. Grill the hens over hot coals or roast in oven at 350°F for 35–40 minutes, turning once or twice, until the birds are golden and crisp on the outside, juicy within, about 20 minutes in total on the barbecue.

5. Serve the poussin garnished with the red pepper-chipotle cream and a sprinkling of cilantro and/or green onion.

NUTRITIONAL INFORMATION				
	TOTAL FAT	SAT FAT	CHOL	ENERGY
Total	154g	65g	855mg	2396kcals
Per Serving	38.5g	16g	214mg	599kcals

PESCADO CHIPOTLE CON SALSA DE
CALABACITAS Y CREMA ACIDA

CHIPOTLE-GRILLED SALMON

WITH THREE-SQUASH SALSA AND SOUR CREAM

SERVES 4

4 salmon steaks or fillets, each 6–8oz.	salt and black pepper
2tbsp. olive oil	1 zucchini, finely diced
dash of ground allspice	1½ cups finely diced yellow squash
dash of ground cinnamon	1½ cups finely diced pale green squash, such as patty pan
juice of 1 lime	
1–2tsp. chipotle marinade or chipotle en adobo sauce or 1 dried chipotle, rehydrated and puréed (page 8)	½ onion, finely chopped
	1–2 tomatoes, diced
	¼tsp. ground cumin
4 cloves garlic, chopped	2tsp. chopped fresh marjoram or oregano
¼tsp. cumin	sour cream, to serve

1. Combine the salmon with half the olive oil, the allspice, cinnamon, half the lime juice, the chipotle marinade or adobo, half the garlic, cumin, salt, and pepper. Let marinate for 30–60 minutes.

2. Meanwhile, make the salsa: cook the zucchini and squash in boiling water or a steamer until just al dente. Drain and toss with the remaining oil and lime juice, the remaining garlic, the onion, tomatoes, cumin, and marjoram or fresh oregano. Set aside.

3. Grill the salmon over hot coals until just cooked through, 3–4 minutes each side, then serve each portion with 1–2tbsp salsa and a dab of sour cream.

NUTRITIONAL INFORMATION				
	TOTAL FAT	SAT FAT	CHOL	ENERGY
Total	100g	16.5g	350mg	1581kcals
Per Serving	25g	4g	88mg	395kcals

CAMARONES TROPICALES A LA PARILLA

RED CHILI-SEASONED SHRIMP

WITH TROPICAL FRUIT

Keeping the shells on the shrimp during their cooking keeps the little creatures succulent and juicy, though they are a bit messy to eat. Provide a little dish for the shells and warm cloths to wash chili-stained fingertips.

SERVES 4

1½lb. shrimp in their shells	¼tsp. ground cumin
1tbsp. achiote seeds, ground or puréed (page 19)	**TO GARNISH**
3tbsp. mild chili powder	handful of bitter salad greens such as chicory
1tbsp. sweet paprika	1 ripe mango, peeled and diced or sliced
5 cloves garlic, chopped	1 ripe papaya, peeled and seeded, cut into the same size as the mango
1tsp. salt	
2tbsp. olive oil	
juice of 1 orange	1 lime, cut into wedges
juice of 1 lime	handful of fresh cilantro leaves or fresh mint leaves or both
dash of dried oregano	

1. Combine the shrimp with the achiote, chili powder, paprika, garlic, salt, olive oil, orange and lime juice, oregano, and cumin. Let marinate for at least 30 minutes.

2. Thread on to skewers and grill over hot coals just long enough to cook through but not overcook, about 2–3 minutes per side.

3. Serve on a platter garnished with chicory, mango, papaya, lime wedges, and cilantro and/or mint leaves.

NUTRITIONAL INFORMATION				
	TOTAL FAT	SAT FAT	CHOL	ENERGY
Total	25g	4g	788mg	627kcals
Per Serving	6g	1g	197mg	157kcals

LANGOSTA A LA PARILLA

LOBSTER COOKED ON THE GRILL AS IN ROSARITA BEACH

Cooking lobsters on the coals gives them a lovely smoky scent that is enhanced by the spicy red chili. Serve with creamy frijoles refritos, soft warm corn tortillas, wedges of lime, and a salsa of choice.

Rosarita Beach near Ensenada in Mexico's Baja California is known for its lobster. In the heyday of Hollywood, before the jet made travel so accessible, Ensenada was a weekend getaway for film stars and directors. The exquisitely fresh lobsters that were hauled from the depths of the sea were also part of the allure: grilled over hot coals, then eaten with warm beans, corn tortillas, and chili salsa.

The spicy butter-basted lobster can be baked instead of barbecued: slather it with the butter and place in a hot oven until it sizzles and is warmed through.

SERVES 4

½ cup butter, softened

4 cloves garlic, chopped

2–4tsp. mild chili powder

3–5tbsp. chopped fresh cilantro

juice of ½ lime or lemon

salt and pepper

2 lobsters, cut through the middle into two halves, or 4 lobster tails, the meat loosened slightly from its shell

1. Mix the butter with the garlic, chili powder, cilantro, lime or lemon juice, and salt and pepper.

2. Spread on to the cut side of the lobster or lobster tails, getting the spicy butter into all the cracks.

3. Cook on the hot coals, cut side up, preferably covered, so that the top is able to brown lightly. Barbecue for about 15 minutes or until heated through, lightly browned and sizzling. Serve immediately.

NUTRITIONAL INFORMATION				
	TOTAL FAT	SAT FAT	CHOL	ENERGY
Total	108g	69g	688mg	1304kcals
Per Serving	27g	17g	172mg	326kcals

MELLEJONES

BARBECUED MUSSELS IN THEIR SHELLS

Many recipes direct scrubbing mussels to rid them of their beard, but I find that cooking mussels on the barbecue makes this step unnecessary. Soaking in salt water seems to be advantageous, however, as the salt water is similar to the sea and I – perhaps irrationally – think it relaxes the little creatures and results in a more tender dish.

SERVES 4

5 pints mussels in their shells
salt

Salsa de Limon y Cilantro (page 19)

1. Place the mussels in a shallow bowl or pan and fill with water to cover. Sprinkle in a generous amount of salt and leave for up to 30 minutes.

2. Place the mussels on a medium low barbecue, and cook, preferably covered, until the mussels pop open, about 10 minutes.

3. Serve the mussels along with the salsa.

NUTRITIONAL INFORMATION				
	TOTAL FAT	SAT FAT	CHOL	ENERGY
Total	15g	2.2g	320mg	808kcals
Per Serving	3.75g	0.5g	80mg	202kcals

VARIATION
BARBECUED CLAMS WITH SALSA

Use clams instead of mussels. Salsa de Muchos Chilles y Jitomates (page 18) is good in addition to the cilantro salsa.

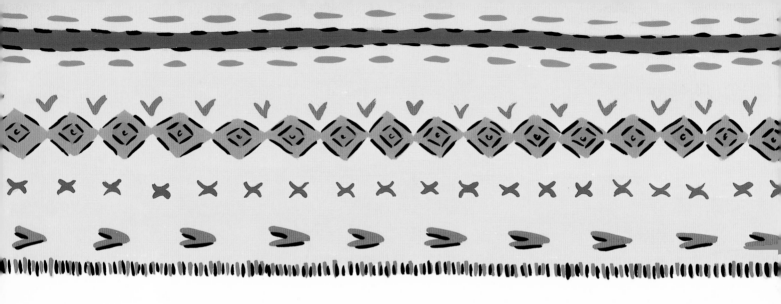

CHAPTER FIVE

BRAISED, STEWED, AND ROASTED DISHES

★ ★ ★ ★ ★

SOUPS AND STEWS

The Mexican kitchen is rich with hearty main-course soups: dishes that exude
the aroma of comfort, some so thick you can leave a spoon standing up in them.
Soup-stews such as posole, birria, and menudo are rumored to cure the eater of
all maladies, ranging from a hangover to sexual impairment!

BIRRIA

STEAMED LAMB
SERVED WITH A SAVORY BROTH

While the original birria is made by wrapping maguey leaves
around the lamb and sealing the pot with a paste of masa and
water, I find that the more easily obtained corn husks trap
plenty of steam in the pot above the meat and give the meat a
subtle corn-scented aroma as well as eliminating the need to
seal the pot with masa paste.

SERVES 4–6

2½–3lb. lamb	½–1tsp. dried oregano, crumbled
1 quantity Recado Rojo (page 18)	4½ cups chicken stock
about 25 corn husks	**TO GARNISH**
1 medium onion, diced	3tbsp. chopped fresh cilantro
5 cloves garlic, chopped	1 small onion, chopped
14oz. tomatoes	1 lime, cut into wedges
2tbsp. olive oil	
salt and pepper	

1. Coat the lamb in the Recado Rojo.
2. Soften the corn husks by pouring boiling water over them
and leaving them, covered, for 30 minutes.
3. Place the lamb in a steamer with water or stock on the
bottom. Cover the meat lightly with wet corn husks so that
they fill the top part of the steamer pot.
4. Steam the meat over a very low heat until very tender,
about 2 hours. Make sure that enough liquid remains at the
bottom of the pot.
5. Meanwhile, purée the onion with the garlic and tomatoes
in a blender or food processor.

6. Heat the oil in a saucepan and when nearly smoking add
the onion-tomato purée. Cook until it changes color and
becomes less watery. Season with salt, pepper, and oregano.
7. Add the stock and bring to a boil. Reduce the heat and
simmer for 10 minutes.
8. Remove the corn husks from the meat, then remove the
meat from the pan. Pour the juices from the bottom of the pan
into the soup.
9. Cut the meat into small pieces and place in warm bowls.
Ladle the soup over it and garnish with cilantro, onion, and
wedges of lime.

NUTRITIONAL INFORMATION

	TOTAL FAT	SAT FAT	CHOL	ENERGY
Total	168g	68g	1185mg	3085kcals
Per Serving (4)	42g	17g	296mg	771kcals
Per Serving (6)	28g	11.5g	198mg	514kcals

VARIATION

I like to serve birria with noodles, garbanzo beans or pinto
beans, and zucchini to give substance and texture to the soup.
Cook chopped zucchini in the simmering soup; thin noodles
should be cooked separately and beans warmed in the soup
with the meat and zucchini. To serve: place some noodles,
zucchini and beans in each bowl then ladle hot soup and lamb
over them. Garnish as suggested.

SOPA DE FRIJOLES CON CHIPOTLE Y LIMON

TARASCAN BEAN STEW
WITH CHIPOTLE AND LEMON

This spicy, lemony bean stew is one of my favorite vegetarian dishes, especially on a winter's night with a chunk of cheese oozing into delicious molten strings at the bottom of my bowl.

SERVES 4-6

½tsp. cumin seeds	4¼ cups vegetable stock
1 onion, chopped	¼tsp. oregano, crushed
1tbsp. olive oil	**TO SERVE**
3–5 cloves garlic, chopped	chipotle en adobo marinade to taste
2 cups cooked drained beans, large white or pink such as pinto	1 lemon, cut into wedges
1¾ cups canned or fresh tomatoes, diced	

1. Toast the cumin seeds in an ungreased heavy-based skillet until they are fragrant and lightly changed in color. Take care they do not burn. Remove from the heat and crush. Set aside.
2. Lightly fry the onion in the olive oil until softened, then add the garlic and cook for a moment longer until fragrant but not browned.
3. Stir in the beans and tomatoes, cook in the fragrant oil for 1–2 minutes, then add the stock and simmer for 15–20 minutes. Remove about half the beans and mash or purée them, then return to the soup; season with oregano and toasted cumin seeds.
4. Serve the soup with a drizzle of chipotle marinade and a squeeze of lemon as desired.

NUTRITIONAL INFORMATION

	TOTAL FAT	SAT FAT	CHOL	ENERGY
Total	14g	2g	0mg	724kcals
Per Serving (4)	3.5g	0.5g	0mg	181kcals
Per Serving (6)	2.3g	0.3g	0mg	121kcals

POLLO TROPICALE

CARIBBEAN-STYLE CHICKEN AND VEGETABLE SOUP-STEW

A sprinkling of diced tomato and banana along with coconut and achiote give this unusual stew a decidedly tropical flavor. I've eaten similar soup-stews along the Caribbean coast, with seafood and fish instead of chicken.

SERVES 4-6

2 mild, fruity, smooth red chilis	3oz. creamed coconut, cut or scraped into small pieces
1 onion, unpeeled, halved	6–8oz. cooked chicken chunks or diced raw chicken breast
5 cloves garlic, unpeeled and whole	large dash of dried oregano
2tsp. achiote seeds ground to a powder or 1tbsp. achiote paste, made by simmering and puréeing the seeds	dash of ground cumin
	salt and pepper
7–8 canned or fresh ripe tomatoes	**TO SERVE**
1tbsp. oil	½ ripe but firm banana
3 cups chicken stock	juice from ½ a lime
1 zucchini, cut into bite-sized pieces	1 lime, cut into wedges
1 cup corn kernels	1tbsp. chopped fresh cilantro
	1 medium tomato, diced

1. Place the chilis in a bowl and pour hot water over them. Let rest until they soften, about 30 minutes. When softened, remove the stems and seeds, then cut the flesh into small pieces. Purée in a blender or food processor, using just enough of the soaking liquid to make a purée.
2. Meanwhile, toast the onion and garlic under the broiler until they are lightly charred.
3. When cool enough to handle, peel the onion and garlic, then dice and combine the achiote seeds and half the tomatoes. Purée in a blender or food processor.
4. Heat the oil in saucepan; when hot, pour in the puréed sauce and cook down until it is concentrated, paste-like, and darkened in color. Do not let it burn.

5. Add the chicken stock and zucchini. Bring to a boil then reduce the heat and cook until the zucchini is cooked through.

6. Add the corn kernels, creamed coconut, chicken chunks, oregano, and cumin and heat through. Stir every so often so that the creamed coconut melts. Add salt and pepper to taste.

7. Just before serving, dice the banana and toss with lime juice. Serve each bowlful of hot soup in a bowl with a sprinkling of banana, cilantro, diced tomato, and wedges of lime. Offer hot pepper seasoning as desired.

NUTRITIONAL INFORMATION

	TOTAL FAT	SAT FAT	CHOL	ENERGY
Total	83g	58g	75mg	1339kcals
Per Serving (4)	21g	14.5g	19mg	335kcals
Per Serving (6)	14g	9.5g	13mg	223kcals

CARNES, AVES Y PESCADOS

BRAISED, STEWED, AND ROASTED DISHES

POLLO CON VERDOLAGAS EN CHILE ROJO

CHILI AND PURSLANE CHICKEN

SERVES 4

1 chicken, cut into serving pieces

juice of 1 lime

2 cloves garlic, chopped

¼tsp. dried oregano

¼tsp. dried marjoram

¼tsp. dried thyme

¼tsp. ground cumin

5 guajillo chilis, toasted and seeded, stems removed

4 pasilla chilis, toasted and seeded, stems removed

2 cups boiling chicken stock

3tbsp. olive oil

1½lb. tomatoes, toasted and lightly charred (page 8)

2 heads of garlic, broken into cloves and peeled

1 bay leaf

4tbsp. masa harina or 2 tortillas

handful of purslane or watercress

1. Rub the chicken with the lime juice, chopped garlic, oregano, marjoram, thyme, cumin, and salt to taste. Leave for at least 1 hour.

2. Place the toasted chilis in a saucepan and pour the boiling stock over them. Cover and leave to rehydrate for 30 minutes or until they soften. Whirl the chilis, and just enough liquid as needed, in a blender or food processor until puréed.

3. Heat 1tbsp. oil then pour in the chili purée and cook until thickened and paste-like. Pour in the remaining soaking stock, simmer for a few minutes then set aside.

4. Brown the chicken pieces then arrange in a baking dish. Add any leftover juices from the marinade and the chili sauce. Cover and simmer over low heat until the chicken is tender, about 25 minutes. (Breasts will cook quickly, dark meat will take longer. If desired, leave the breasts out for 10 minutes while dark meat cooks.)

5. Toast the masa harina in an ungreased heavy-based skillet or toast the tortillas in the same manner and grind in a blender or food processor. Stir the toasted masa harina or ground tortillas into the sauce, adjusting the seasoning with a squirt of lime if needed and more stock if the sauce is too thick.

6. Just before serving, stir in the purslane or sprinkle with watercress.

NUTRITIONAL INFORMATION

	TOTAL FAT	SAT FAT	CHOL	ENERGY
Total	81.6g	18.75g	630mg	1979kcals
Per Serving	20g	4.5g	158mg	495kcals

62

POLLO DEL JARDIN DE SAN MARCOS
SAN MARCOS CHICKEN

Aguascalientes, a small state in the center of Mexico, is renowned for its fruit and vegetables, as well as the annual fête held in the Garden of San Marcos, in the capital city of the region.

SERVES 4

2tbsp. olive oil

1 chicken, cut into serving pieces

1 onion, finely chopped

5 cloves garlic, chopped

1½lb. tomatoes, diced

2 cups chicken stock

3–4tbsp. vinegar

large dash of sugar

large dash of ground cloves

salt and pepper

¼tsp. dried oregano or marjoram

2–3 large potatoes, part-cooked or steamed until half cooked then peeled and cut into slices or chunks

2 chorizos, skinned and broken into small pieces

1 Romaine lettuce

2 onions, finely chopped

1tsp. capers

pickled jalapeño or serrano chilis (optional)

1. Heat the olive oil in a skillet and lightly fry the chicken with 1 chopped onion and the garlic until the chicken is lightly golden and half-cooked. Remove from the heat.
2. In a blender or food processor, purée the tomatoes with the stock, vinegar, sugar, cloves, salt and pepper, oregano or marjoram. Place in a saucepan and bring to a boil. Reduce the heat and keep on a low simmer. Spoon about a third of the sauce over the chicken and return the chicken to the heat to finish cooking, covered, for another 15–25 minutes or so. If the chicken threatens to burn, add a little more oil or sauce.
3. Meanwhile, brown the potatoes with the chorizo.
4. Serve the cooked chicken on lettuce leaves, each portion with a spoonful or two of the potatoes and chorizo, chopped onion, capers, and pickled jalapeño or serrano chilis if using.

NUTRITIONAL INFORMATION

	TOTAL FAT	SAT FAT	CHOL	ENERGY
Total	119.5g	37g	710mg	2451kcals
Per Serving	30g	9g	178mg	613kcals

CHILI CHICKEN
WITH ROASTED GREEN PEPPER

SERVES 4

6 smooth-skinned mild red chilis	⅛tsp. dried thyme
1½ onions, toasted in an ungreased heavy-based skillet	2tbsp. olive oil
12–15 cloves garlic, toasted in an ungreased heavy-based skillet	½tsp. salt
1tbsp. ground achiote (page 19)	1 fresh or canned tomato, chopped
⅛–¼tsp. ground cinnamon	4 boneless, skinless half chicken breasts, cut into strips
large dash of ground cumin	3–4 onions, quartered
large dash of black pepper	2 green bell peppers, roasted, peeled, and cut into strips
small dash of ground cloves	1 lime, cut into wedges
2tbsp. vinegar	fresh salsa of choice

1. Toast the chilis over an open flame until they catch fire. Let them burn for just a moment then blow out the flame. You want the chilis just slightly charred.

2. Remove the stems from the chilis and discard the seeds. Break the chilis into small pieces, place in a blender or food processor and purée with the toasted onions, garlic, achiote, cinnamon, cumin, black pepper, cloves, vinegar, thyme, half the olive oil, salt, and tomato. Whirl until the mixture forms a paste.

3. Coat the chicken with the spice paste and leave to marinate for about 30 minutes.

4. In an ungreased heavy-based skillet, lightly char the onion quarters, then remove from the pan. Add the remaining olive oil and fry the chicken strips, letting them cook quickly but not overcook. Remove from the pan. Quickly cook the peppers in the same pan then return the onions and chicken and warm through. Serve immediately, with lime and fresh salsa.

NUTRITIONAL INFORMATION

	TOTAL FAT	SAT FAT	CHOL	ENERGY
Total	37g	7.5g	172mg	892kcals
Per Serving	9g	2g	43mg	223kcals

POLLO CON NOPALES Y CHILE ROJO
CHICKEN AND CACTUS
WITH RED CHILI-GARLIC OIL

Marinating the chicken gives it flavor; poaching keeps it light, and the final tiny drizzle of chili and garlic-infused oil gives it extra oomph.

This dish was inspired by the contemporary dishes coming out of Mexico these days: traditional ingredients and preparations with new thoughts and ideas, much in the same way the French kitchen went through changes in the 1970s and 1980s.

SERVES 4

1 chicken, cut into serving pieces, or 4–8 half chicken breasts on the bone

1 quantity chili-achiote seasoning paste from Pollo Rojo (page 50)

1 smooth-skinned flavorful dried chili, crumbled

3tbsp. olive oil

1 clove garlic, thinly sliced

3 cups chicken stock

1 onion, halved and toasted

2–3 tomatoes, diced

8oz. cooked, drained cactus, cut into strips

1. Coat the chicken with seasoning paste. Make incisions all over the bird to ensure the seasonings really flavor the flesh. Let marinate overnight in the refrigerator.
2. To make the chili oil, heat the chili in a saucepan with the olive oil until small bubbles form at the edge of the pan. Remove from the heat and add the garlic. Let cool to room temperature, then strain. Set aside.
3. Bring the stock, onion, and tomatoes to a boil in a large pan then reduce the heat. Add the chicken and simmer, covered, over a low heat, until tender, about 10 minutes for chicken breasts, 30 minutes for a whole chicken.
4. Serve the poached chicken in a bowl with the cactus and a little of the liquid puddled around it. Drizzle with a small amount of the red chili-garlic oil and serve immediately.

NUTRITIONAL INFORMATION				
	TOTAL FAT	SAT FAT	CHOL	ENERGY
Total	80g	18.5g	630mg	1692 kcals
Per Serving	20g	4.5g	158mg	423kcals

POLLO Y ELOTE SUIZA
CHICKEN AND CORN
IN CREAMY CHILI-TOMATO SAUCE

This creamy chicken dish is called Suiza (Swiss) because of the crème fraîche sauce – at one time anything that contained cream in Mexico was thought to have originated in Switzerland.

SERVES 4

1 chicken, cut into serving pieces

1tsp. ground cumin

salt and pepper

1–2tbsp. olive oil

5 cloves garlic, minced or chopped

½–1 fresh red chili such as jalapeño, thinly sliced

3 green onions, thinly sliced

1¾ cups tomatoes, diced

1 cup chicken stock

2 bay leaves

1¼ cups canned corn kernels, drained

1½ cups crème fraîche or sour cream

1. Rub the chicken with cumin, salt and pepper, and olive oil.
2. Heat an ungreased heavy-based skillet and lightly brown the chicken, using the extra oil from rubbing it.
3. Add the garlic, red chili and green onions, then cover and cook over medium-low heat for about 10 minutes.
4. Add the tomatoes, cover, and continue to simmer until the chicken is cooked through, about 25 minutes.
5. Remove the chicken from the pan and place on a plate. Keep warm while you finish the sauce.
6. In a blender or food processor, purée the sauce with the chicken stock. Heat the remaining oil in a skillet then pour in the puréed sauce, bay leaves, and corn. Cook over high heat for about 5 minutes to reduce the sauce a little.
7. Stir in the crème fraîche or sour cream, then return the chicken to the pan along with any juices that have accumulated. Season with salt and pepper and warm through.
8. Serve hot, with a few spoonfuls of sauce.

NUTRITIONAL INFORMATION				
	TOTAL FAT	SAT FAT	CHOL	ENERGY
Total	133g	62g	855mg	2417kcals
Per Serving	33g	15.5g	214mg	604kcals

BRAISED, STEWED, AND ROASTED DISHES

PICADILLO

SPICY-SWEET MEAT HASH
WITH ALMONDS AND GREEN OLIVES

Use picadillo to stuff into roasted green chilis for superb chilis rellenos, or roll a warm wheat tortilla around several spoonfuls of hot picadillo and a ladleful of black or red beans. Picadillo makes an excellent filling for empanadas, especially easily made empanadas using the very inauthentic but delicious filo dough for the pastry.

SERVES 6

4 cups lean ground beef

2tbsp. vegetable oil, if needed

1–2 large onions, chopped

5 cloves garlic, chopped

½tsp. dried oregano

½tsp. ground cinnamon

¼tsp. ground cloves

8 fresh or canned tomatoes, diced or chopped

2–3tbsp. sugar

2–3 fresh green chilis, chopped

1–2tbsp. vinegar

¾ cup sherry

½–⅔ cup raisins

¾ cup green pimento-stuffed olives, sliced or halved

¾–1 cup toasted almonds, coarsely chopped or slivered

3–4tbsp. chopped fresh cilantro

1. Fry the beef and onion until lightly browned. Add oil if needed, then stir in the onions, garlic, oregano, cinnamon, cloves, and tomatoes and continue to cook for a few minutes longer.

2. Add the sugar, chilis, vinegar, sherry, and raisins and cook over high heat until the liquid has evaporated by at least half.

3. Stir in the olives, almonds, and cilantro, taste for seasoning, and serve immediately.

NUTRITIONAL INFORMATION				
	TOTAL FAT	SAT FAT	CHOL	ENERGY
Total	137g	29g	590mg	2929kcals
Per Serving (6)	23g	5g	98mg	488kcals
Per Serving (8)	17g	3.5g	74mg	366kcals

POLLO CON SALSA DE CIRUELA

CHICKEN WITH PRUNES

Prunes make a rich, winey sauce, their sweetness balanced with the spicy, smoky chipotle chili and the tangy edge of tamarind. Serve with boiled potatoes sprinkled with cumin and green onions, or with steamed rice tossed with strips of roasted peeled green peppers and sautéed onions, with a sprinkling of cumin.

SERVES 4

1 chicken, cut into serving pieces

juice of ½ lime or 4–6 crushed cooked tomatillos

5 cloves garlic, chopped

chipotle salsa or marinade from chipotle chilis, to taste

salt and pepper

flour for dusting

vegetable oil

6–8 tomatoes, diced

1 onion, chopped

½ cup wine, beer or brandy

1½ cups chicken stock

10–12 prunes, pitted

2–3tbsp. sugar or honey

1tbsp. tamarind paste or Worcestershire sauce to taste

½tsp. ground cinnamon

¼tsp. ground allspice or large dash of ground cloves

vinegar

TO GARNISH

2tbsp. lightly toasted flaked almonds

1tbsp. chopped fresh cilantro

1. Combine the chicken with the lime juice or tomatillos, half the garlic, the chipotle salsa, and salt and pepper. Let marinate for 1 hour to overnight.

2. Dust the chicken with flour then lightly brown in oil in a skillet, taking care it does not burn. Place in a casserole then pour out the fat from the skillet.

3. Add the tomatoes, onion, wine, beer or brandy, chicken stock, and remaining garlic to the skillet, and bring to a boil. Simmer for a few minutes until the onion turns translucent, then add the prunes, sugar or honey, tamarind paste or Worcestershire sauce, cinnamon, cloves, and chipotle to taste.

4. Pour the sauce into the casserole, letting it lightly coat the chicken and sink to the bottom of the casserole. Place the prunes under the chicken.

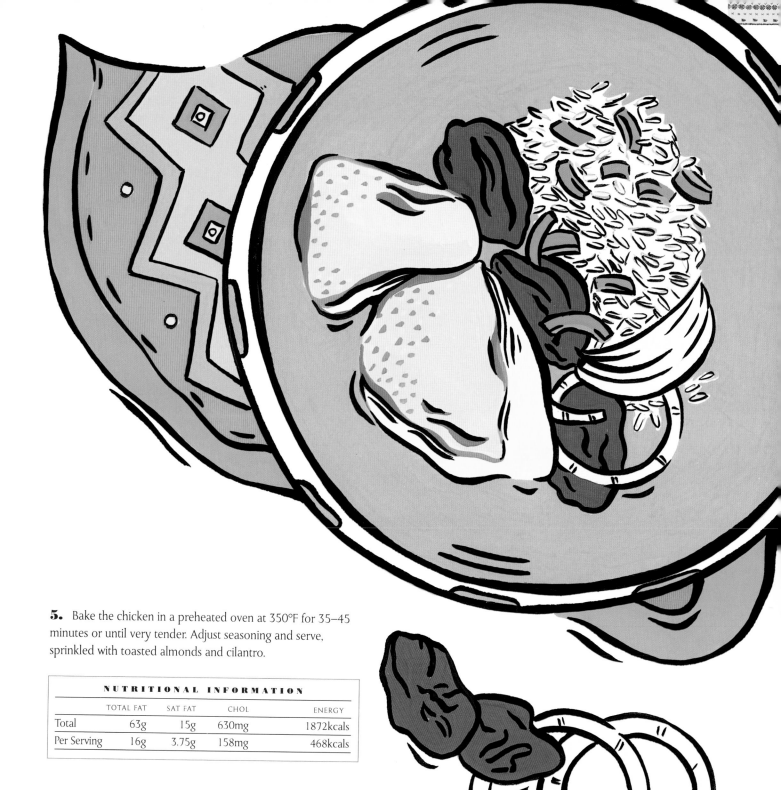

5. Bake the chicken in a preheated oven at 350°F for 35–45 minutes or until very tender. Adjust seasoning and serve, sprinkled with toasted almonds and cilantro.

NUTRITIONAL INFORMATION				
	TOTAL FAT	SAT FAT	CHOL	ENERGY
Total	63g	15g	630mg	1872kcals
Per Serving	16g	3.75g	158mg	468kcals

MANCHAMANTEL

CHICKEN AND/OR PORK
IN MANCHAMANTEL SAUCE

Manchamantel is a type of bright red, fruit-redolent sauce, used for simmering chicken and/or pork. Its name translates as "tablecloth stainer" – perhaps because of its lurid color, perhaps because in the enthusiasm of the moment, diners tend to spill a lot of the lovely sauce as they aim for their mouths. Manchamantel sauce can be prepared without the chicken or meat and used with foods grilled over coals: the richness of duck especially is nice with the fruity sauce.

SERVES 4

2 ancho chilis	1–2tsp. sugar
1 guajillo chili	1lb. boneless pork and ½ chicken, in serving pieces, or 2lb. pork, or 1 chicken
2 cups hot water	
½ onion, toasted	1 zucchini or chayote, cut into bite-sized pieces
3 cloves garlic, toasted	
4 tomatoes, toasted and lightly charred	1 apple, preferably tart, peeled, cored and diced
1 cup meat or chicken stock, or ½–1 bouillon cube mixed with water	½ carrot, thinly sliced
	dried fruit: several tablespoons raisins, several prunes, a dried pear, apple, and apricot (optional)
½tsp. ground cinnamon	
⅛tsp. ground cloves	
salt and pepper	½ ripe pineapple, peeled and cut into bite-sized chunks
1–2tbsp. oil	
1–2tbsp. vinegar	1 banana, diced

1. Toast the chilis on an open flame until they turn color but do not blacken. Place in a pan of hot water and simmer for 20 minutes or until the chilis are softened.

2. Remove the stems and seeds and, in a blender or food processor, purée the chilis with enough of their soaking liquid to make a smooth purée.

3. Skin roast the onion and garlic (page 8) and dice; dice the tomatoes (leave on their charred skin – it adds flavor). Add the onion, garlic and tomatoes to the chili purée and whirl to make a smooth sauce. Season with cinnamon, cloves, and salt and pepper.

4. Heat the oil and when it is almost smoking pour in the sauce. Cook for a few minutes until it concentrates and darkens slightly, then add the vinegar, sugar, and pork if using both pork and chicken. If using only chicken, add that now.

5. Cook for about 45 minutes then add chicken and simmer a further 20–30 minutes.

6. Add the zucchini or chayote, apple, carrot, dried fruit, if using, and pineapple. Continue to simmer until the fruit and meat are tender.

7. Adjust the seasoning and sugar-vinegar balance, then add the banana and warm through. Serve immediately.

NUTRITIONAL INFORMATION				
	TOTAL FAT	SAT FAT	CHOL	ENERGY
Total	72g	21g	660mg	2187kcals
Per Serving	18g	5g	165mg	547kcals

ALBONDIGAS CON CALABACITAS EN SALSA VERDE

MEATBALLS WITH ZUCCHINI AND POTATOES
IN GREEN TOMATILLO SAUCE

SERVES 4

1lb. lean ground beef	1½ cups tomatillos, cooked and drained
6tbsp. cooked, drained rice or soft bread crumbs	1–2 fresh green chilis such as serrano
1 egg, lightly beaten	dash of ground turmeric
½ onion, finely chopped	1tbsp. vinegar
3 cloves garlic, chopped	2tbsp. vegetable oil
3–4tbsp. chopped fresh cilantro	2 cups chicken or beef stock
4 guajillo chilis, toasted, seeded, stemmed, and ground	1–2 large baking potatoes, peeled and cut into chunks
	2–3 zucchini, sliced
½tsp. ground cumin plus a dash for the tomatillo sauce	TO SERVE
salt and pepper	3tbsp. fresh cilantro
	wedges of lemon or lime

1. Combine the meat with the rice or bread crumbs, egg, onion, half the garlic, the chopped cilantro, ground chili powder, cumin, and salt and pepper to taste. Roll into meatballs and set aside.

2. In a blender or food processor, purée the tomatillos with the remaining garlic, fresh chili, dash of cumin, turmeric, and vinegar.

3. Heat the oil in a saucepan; when hot pour in the tomatillo mixture and cook until it reduces in volume and becomes a paste-like mixture.

4. Add the stock, potato, and zucchini and carefully place the meatballs in the mixture. Cover and simmer over low heat for 20–30 minutes or until the vegetables are cooked through, occasionally basting the meatballs with the sauce. Taste for salt and pepper.

5. Serve in bowls, each sprinkled with cilantro and accompanied by a wedge of lemon or lime.

NUTRITIONAL INFORMATION				
	TOTAL FAT	SAT FAT	CHOL	ENERGY
Total	55.5g	14.5g	533mg	1536kcals
Per Serving	14g	3.75g	133mg	384kcals

ALBONDIGAS EN SALSA ROJO CON LEGUMBRES

MEATBALLS IN SWEET-SPICY RED CHILI SAUCE
WITH ASSORTED VEGETABLES

SERVES 4

1 cup each of ground pork and ground beef, or all ground beef

6tbsp. cooked, drained rice or 3–4tbsp. masa harina

1 egg, lightly beaten

1½ onions, finely chopped

3 cloves garlic, chopped

½tsp. ground cumin

1½ cups stock

⅛–¼tsp. ground cinnamon

2tbsp. currants or raisins

½tbsp. dark brown sugar

1–2tbsp. vinegar

1 sweet potato, peeled and cut into chunks, or 2inch slice of pumpkin, peeled and cut into chunks

1tsp. chopped fresh parsley

1tbsp. chopped fresh mint

large dash of dried thyme

large dash of ground cloves

salt and pepper

6 fresh or canned tomatoes

3tbsp. ancho chili powder

2tbsp. vegetable oil

1 zucchini or chayote, cut into chunks (if using chayote, peel and seed)

¼ cabbage, cut into chunks and blanched or part-cooked

1tbsp. chipotle salsa or marinade from chipotles en adobo (optional)

2–3tbsp. chopped fresh cilantro

1. Mix the ground meat with the rice or bread crumbs, egg, half the onion, half the garlic, and the parsley, cumin and mint and season with thyme, cloves, and salt and pepper. Roll into egg-shaped meatballs and set aside.

2. In a blender or food processor, purée the tomatoes with the chili powder and remaining onion and garlic. Heat the oil in a skillet then pour in the puréed tomato-onion mixture and cook until it reduces and darkens slightly.

3. Add the stock, cinnamon, currants or raisins, brown sugar, vinegar, sweet potato or pumpkin, zucchini or chayote and cabbage and mix well. Bring to a boil then reduce the heat to very low.

4. Gently place the meatballs in the mixture, cover, and simmer gently for 20–30 minutes, basting the meatballs occasionally with the sauce.

5. Adjust the seasoning of vinegar and brown sugar, check for salt, and add a little chili powder or chipotle salsa or marinade to taste. Serve hot, in bowls, sprinkled with cilantro, accompanied by either rice or tortillas.

NUTRITIONAL INFORMATION				
	TOTAL FAT	SAT FAT	CHOL	ENERGY
Total	62g	16g	558mg	1747kcals
Per Serving	15.5g	4g	139mg	437kcals

POLLO DE PLAZA ESTILO MORELIA

CHICKEN FROM THE PLAZA IN MORELIA

Surrounding the plaza in the colonial town of Morelia, vendors and restaurants offer pollo de plaza, a savory concoction of chicken and enchiladas bathed in two sauces: red chili and tomato.

SERVES 4

4 half chicken breasts, on the bone	large dash of ground allspice
½tsp. dried thyme	large dash of ground cumin
18 cloves garlic, chopped	vegetable oil
salt and pepper	1½lb. fresh or canned tomatoes, diced
2 bay leaves, crushed into a fine powder	12 tortillas
3–4 pasilla, ancho, or negro chilis	**TO SERVE**
1 onion, chopped	shredded Romaine lettuce
¼ cup vinegar	chopped onion
1 cup boiling water	crumbled dried oregano
2 onions, chopped	crumbled Feta cheese
1tsp. dried oregano	fresh serrano or jalapeño chili, thinly sliced
large dash of ground cinnamon	diced cooked carrots
	diced cooked potatoes

1. Coat the chicken with thyme, one-third of the garlic, salt and pepper, and bay leaves. Set aside.

2. To make the chili sauce, toast the chilis in an ungreased heavy-based skillet until they change color slightly then remove the seeds and stems. Combine with the vinegar and water and let soften for 30 minutes.

3. Place the chilis in a blender or food processor with half the onion, one-third of the garlic, the oregano, cinnamon, allspice and cumin, and the soaking liquid. Whirl until the mixture forms a smooth sauce consistency.

4. Heat two tablespoons oil and pour in the chili mixture. Cook over high heat until it reduces in volume and intensifies in flavor. Adjust the seasoning and set aside.

5. To make the tomato sauce, whirl the tomatoes, remaining onion and remaining garlic in a blender or food processor until smooth. Heat 2 tbsp. oil in a skillet and pour in the tomato mixture; season with sugar and salt and pepper to taste and cook until thickened and flavorful. Set aside.

6. Roast the chicken breasts in a casserole in a preheated oven at 325°F for about 15 minutes or pan brown in 1–2 tbsp. oil.

7. To make the enchiladas, warm the tortillas in a small amount of oil then dip each one into the hot chili sauce. Roll up immediately, arrange in a casserole and keep warm.

8. Serve the chicken sauced with a little tomato sauce, surrounded by enchiladas and chili sauce, garnished with lettuce, onion, oregano, Feta cheese, fresh chili, carrots, and potatoes.

NUTRITIONAL INFORMATION				
	TOTAL FAT	SAT FAT	CHOL	ENERGY
Total	22g	5g	172mg	2297kcals
Per Serving	5.5g	1g	43mg	574kcals

PATO A LA NARANJA

DUCK ROASTED WITH ORANGES AND MILD RED CHILI

SERVES 4

1 duck, prepared for roasting

salt and pepper

1 orange, washed and halved

1 lime, washed and halved

5–8 whole garlic cloves, unpeeled

4tbsp. Recado Rojo (page 18) (or a paste of mild red chili powder seasoned with garlic, cumin and chopped cilantro, and thinned with a little orange juice)

1 onion, chopped

2 cloves garlic, chopped

3tbsp. chopped fresh cilantro

2 fresh green chilis such as serrano or jalapeño, chopped

juice of 2 oranges, plus about ½tsp. of the grated zest

juice of ½ grapefruit, plus ⅛–¼tsp. of the grated zest

juice of ½ lime

dash of ground cumin

2tbsp. sugar

½ cup chicken, beef, or duck stock

1. Place the duck in a roasting pan and sprinkle with salt and pepper all over. Lightly prick its skin evenly to help the fat drain off. Stuff with the orange and lime halves, whole garlic cloves, and 3tbsp. Recado Rojo.

2. Roast in a preheated oven at 450°F for 20 minutes, then reduce the heat to 325°F and continue to cook for another hour so so or until the temperature reaches 350°F in its thigh. During the roasting, spoon or gently pour off the duck fat as it cooks (roast on a rack for allover crispness and easy draining). Save the duck fat for cooking potatoes and so on.

3. While the duck is cooking, make the salsa: combine the onion, garlic, cilantro, chilis, half the orange juice and the zest, the grapefruit juice and zest, and lime juice. Season with salt and cumin. Set aside.

4. Remove the duck from oven and place on a platter to allow it to settle for carving. Remove the stuffing ingredients and squeeze to extract their juices. Keep warm.

5. Spoon off any fat remaining in the pan. Add the juices from the platter and stuffing to the roasting pan, along with the remaining orange juice, the sugar, and stock. Bring to a boil, stirring all the while to scrape up the crusty brown bits. Adjust the seasoning, adding more sugar or a dash of lime juice as needed.

6. Carve the duck and serve napped with the hot pan sauce and garnished with spoonfuls of the fresh salsa.

NUTRITIONAL INFORMATION				
	TOTAL FAT	SAT FAT	CHOL	ENERGY
Total	257g	70g	0mg	2856kcals
Per Serving	64g	17g	0mg	714kcals

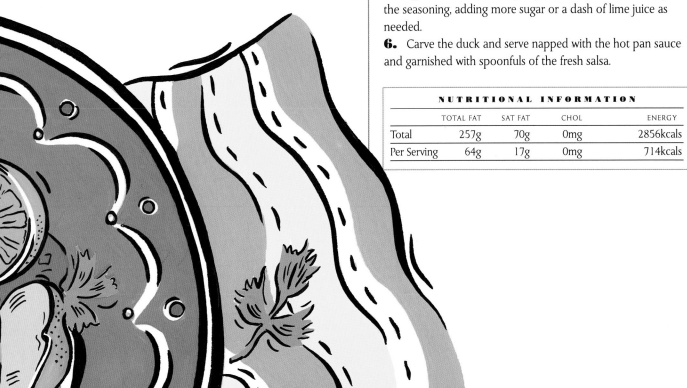

LOMO DE PUERCO

LOIN OF PORK BAKED IN SHARP-SOUR RED CHILI SAUCE

Adobo, a red chili sauce sharpened with vinegar and balanced with just a touch of sugar, is eaten with a variety of foods such as meats, fish, and poultry. It is also often used as a pickling mixture, especially for chipotle, the feisty smoked chili. When meat and fish are prepared en adobo, they are usually first marinated in the mixture, then covered and baked until meltingly tender in the same mixture. This adobo permeates the flesh completely, an especially good technique where meat and poultry are old and tough, as they often are in rural regions of Mexico.

SERVES 4

4 large ancho chilis	dash of ground allspice or cloves
2 cups hot stock	1tbsp. sugar
1tsp. ground cumin	2lb. loin of pork
several sprigs of fresh thyme	salt and pepper
¼tsp. dried oregano	
5–8 cloves garlic, chopped	**TO SERVE**
3tbsp. orange juice	salsa of choice
2tbsp. red wine vinegar	chopped fresh cilantro
½–1tsp. chipotle marinade (optional)	sour cream
	warm corn tortillas

1. Lightly toast the chilis over a hot flame until they change color. Remove the stems and seeds and discard, and tear the chili into small pieces, then combine with the hot stock to soften.

2. When the chilis have softened, whirl them in a blender or food processor with cumin, thyme, oregano, garlic, orange juice, vinegar, chipotle marinade, if using, a pinch of allspice or cloves, and sugar.

3. Sprinkle pork with salt and pepper then place in casserole and spoon sauce over it. Seal and roast in a preheated oven at 350°F for 2 hours then uncover and cook for another 30–45 minutes or until browned and crusty on top.

4. Serve with salsa of choice, chopped onions, cilantro, sour cream, and corn tortillas.

NUTRITIONAL INFORMATION				
	TOTAL FAT	SAT FAT	CHOL	ENERGY
Total	53g	19g	518mg	1197kcals
Per Serving	13g	4.5g	129mg	299kcals

CORDERO AL PASTOR

ROAST LAMB
WITH TEQUILA RED CHILI SEASONING, GREEN OLIVES AND CRUMBLED CHEESE

The simple, strong flavors of this dish combine brilliantly. Serve with warm corn tortillas or crusty rolls (bolillos) and a salad of shredded lettuce, roasted mild green chilis, and avocado.

SERVES 4

2–3lb. lamb shoulder	2 cups chicken or beef stock
1tsp. paprika	1–2tsp sugar
1–2tbsp. mild chili powder	
2tsp. ground cumin	**TO GARNISH**
salt and pepper	6–8oz. crumbly cheese such as Queso Fresco, Pecorino, Lancashire, or not-too-salty Feta
6 cloves garlic, chopped	
juice of 1 orange	15 green olives, sliced
juice of 1 lime or lemon	2tbsp. coarsely chopped fresh cilantro
¼ cup tequila	

1. Rub the lamb with the paprika, chili powder, cumin, salt and pepper, half the garlic, the orange and lime or lemon juice and tequila. Let marinate for about an hour.

2. Place the lamb in a roasting pan and pour in half the stock. Place in a preheated oven at 350°F. Cook the lamb until tender, basting from time to time, raising the heat at the end for about 10 minutes so that any fatty areas brown and crisp. Add more stock if the pan drippings threaten to burn or blacken.

3. Remove the lamb from the pan and let rest in a warm place while you make the sauce.

4. Spoon off all fat from the pan drippings, then add the remaining stock, the remaining garlic, and the sugar. Bring to a boil. It should form a savory sauce.

5. Slice the lamb and pour the sauce over it. Garnish with crumbled cheese, olives, and cilantro leaves. Serve immediately.

NUTRITIONAL INFORMATION				
	TOTAL FAT	SAT FAT	CHOL	ENERGY
Total	198g	139g	668mg	2694kcals
Per Serving	50g	35g	167mg	674kcals

LOMITOS

TENDER, SIMMERED, ORANGE-SAFFRON MARINATED PORK

This dish is from the Yucatan, where it is simmered in great cazuelas. In the marketplace in Merida you can buy it warm, served spooned on to fresh tortillas or thick masa cakes. Beef, lamb, or turkey thigh could be used in place of the pork.

SERVES 4-6

2lb. boneless pork, cut into pieces

2tbsp. mild chili powder or mixture of sweet paprika and mild chili

3 cloves garlic, chopped

salt and pepper

3 heads of garlic, unpeeled, cut into halves crosswise, toasted, and lightly charred

1 fresh green chili, lightly charred

¾ cup orange juice

grated zest from ½ orange

2 dashes of saffron

juice of ½ lime

¼tsp. cumin seeds

1tbsp. oil

1 onion, chopped

1 green bell pepper, chopped

1lb. tomatoes, chopped

1 cup water

1. Combine the pork with the chili powder, garlic, orange juice, orange zest, saffron, lime juice, cumin seeds, and salt and pepper. Let marinate in the refrigerator for 3 hours to overnight.

2. Peel the toasted garlic and coarsely chop. Remove the stems and seeds from the toasted chili; peel and coarsely chop. Set aside.

3. Heat the oil in a skillet and fry the onion, green pepper, and tomatoes until the onion softens, then add the reserved garlic, green chili, pork, and water, and simmer on low to medium heat until the meat is very tender and the sauce has evaporated to a thick paste-like sauce.

4. Adjust the seasoning and add a squeeze of orange/lime if needed. Serve immediately, with tortillas or rice and salad.

NUTRITIONAL INFORMATION				
	TOTAL FAT	SAT FAT	CHOL	ENERGY
Total	84.5g	27g	690mg	1810kcals
Per Serving (6)	21g	7g	173mg	452kcals
Per Serving (4)	17g	5g	138mg	362kcals

VARIATION
TACOS DE LOMITOS

Spoon on to homemade tortillas and top with a sprinkling of cilantro and chopped slightly bitter salad greens such as chicory.

ZANCAS DE CARDERO CON POSOLE

ROASTED LAMB SHANKS
POT-ROASTED WITH HOMINY

Rich chili and tomato-spiced lamb, braised until moist and tender, is delicious with gentle hominy, all topped with the crisp freshness of shredded cabbage salad.

SERVES 4

4 lamb shanks or 1 shoulder roast

1 quantity red chili paste, Recado Rojo (page 18)

1 onion, finely chopped

5 tomatoes, diced

1 red bell pepper, chopped

1 green bell pepper, chopped

1 cup chicken or beef stock

½ cup beer

1 lime, cut into wedges

½ cabbage, thinly sliced or shredded

olive oil and vinegar to taste

salt and pepper

12oz. cooked, drained hominy

¼tsp. dried oregano

salsa of choice

1. Make incisions all over the lamb then coat with the red chili paste. Let marinate for at least 1 hour, and preferably overnight.

2. Place in a baking dish and surround with the onion, tomatoes, and red and green peppers. Pour in the stock and beer then cover the dish and bake in a preheated oven at 375°F for 2 hours or until the lamb is tender inside and crusty on the outside.

3. Meanwhile, dress the cabbage with oil and vinegar, salt and pepper, and set aside.

4. Pour off the fat from the baking dish, add the hominy to the pan juices and heat through. Serve the lamb and hominy with the pan juices, cabbage salad, and sprinkling of oregano. Accompany with a salsa of choice.

NUTRITIONAL INFORMATION				
	TOTAL FAT	SAT FAT	CHOL	ENERGY
Total	145g	105g	510mg	3032kcals
Per Serving	36g	26g	128mg	758kcals

COSTILLAS DE PUERCO

ROASTED SPARERIBS

The simplest meats are often the best. These spareribs should be juicy yet crispy, the fat having cooked right out of them, to be drained off.

SERVES 4

3–5lb. spareribs, cut into separate pieces	salsa of choice such as Salsa de Pina (page 15)
salt and pepper	

1. Arrange the meat in a single layer in a baking dish and salt and pepper liberally. Add water to just cover.

2. Bake in a preheated oven at 300–325°F for about 3 hours, or until the water evaporates and the meat becomes crispy. Pour off excess fat every so often as the meat cooks. About 15 minutes before serving, toss with 4tbsp. salsa, then return to the oven.

3. Adjust the seasoning and serve with salsa, tortillas, frijoles, and guacamole.

NUTRITIONAL INFORMATION				
	TOTAL FAT	SAT FAT	CHOL	ENERGY
Total	325g	164g	1080mg	4050kcals
Per Serving	81g	41g	270mg	1013kcals

VARIATION
SPARERIBS AND CLAMS WITH SALSA

Cook the meat as directed above; when it is almost done, add 3–5 clams per person. Toss the meat and clams with 3–5tbsp. homemade mild salsa then raise the heat and return to the oven. Bake at 450°F for 15 minutes or until the clams open. Serve with extra salsa.

CHICHARRON SUDADO EN SALSA VERDE

PORK BELLIES BRAISED IN GREEN SAUCE

This is a typical Tapatio or Guadaljaran dish, at its best when the meat is wrapped into soft tortillas for tacos.

SERVES 4

1½lb. pork belly, without rind, cut Into bite-sized pieces

1 quantity mild Salsa Verde de Tomatillo (page 15)

dash of ground cumin

1 serrano chili, thinly sliced

2tbsp. chopped fresh cilantro

1tbsp. chopped onion

handful of purslane or watercress

1. Arrange the pork with the salsa in a baking dish. Cover and bake in a preheated oven at 325°F hours or until the meat is very tender. Spoon off the excess fat that rises to the surface.
2. Serve hot, sprinkled with cumin, chili, cilantro, onion, and purslane or watercress. Accompany with tortillas.

NUTRITIONAL INFORMATION				
	TOTAL FAT	SAT FAT	CHOL	ENERGY
Total	152g	98g	540mg	2032kcals
Per Serving	38g	24.5g	135mg	508kcals

CALAMARES A LA VERACRUZANA

SQUID SIMMERED WITH TOMATOES, OLIVES, AND CAPERS

Squid is very popular throughout the coastal regions of Mexico, either cooked on the barbecue or simmered with spicy tomato mixtures such as in this dish.

SERVES 4

2lb. cleaned squid, cut into rings and tentacles

2tbsp. olive oil

salt

1 large onion, chopped

3 cloves garlic, chopped

2lb. ripe tomatoes, peeled and chopped (or use canned)

2 fresh green chilis, thinly sliced

1tbsp. chopped fresh parsley

several sprigs of fresh thyme

several sprigs of fresh oregano or marjoram

1 bay leaf

⅛tsp. ground cinnamon

dash of ground allspice

dash of sugar (optional)

1tbsp. capers

15–20 green olives

1tbsp. chopped fresh cilantro

1. Lightly fry the squid in olive oil until it turns opaque. Season with salt and remove to a plate, leaving behind the flavored oil in the pan.
2. Fry the onion and garlic in the squid-scented oil until softened, then stir in the tomatoes, chilis and herbs and season with cinnamon, allspice, and sugar if needed.
3. Cover and cook over medium-low heat until the mixture turns sauce-like and flavorful, about 5 minutes, then uncover the pan and cook for a further 5 minutes.
4. Stir in the reserved squid and any juices, along with the capers and olives. Warm through. Taste for seasoning, then serve immediately, sprinkled with cilantro.

NUTRITIONAL INFORMATION				
	TOTAL FAT	SAT FAT	CHOL	ENERGY
Total	47g	9g	2250mg	1268kcals
Per Serving	12g	2g	563mg	317kcals

PESCADO DE LUJO DE MERIDA

FISH WITH TOMATO-CHIPOTLE CHILI SAUCE

AND PLANTAINS MASHED WITH BACON

SERVES 4

- 4–6 steaks white firm-fleshed fish
- ¼ cup lime juice
- ¼tsp. dried tarragon
- 1–2tbsp. olive oil
- salt and pepper
- 4 tomatoes, roasted in an ungreased pan
- Salsa de Muchos Chilis y Jitomate (page 18)
- ⅛–¼tsp. dried oregano
- ⅛–¼tsp. ground cinnamon
- extra chipotle chili marinade (optional)
- 3–4 ripe but firm plantains, peeled and cut into bite-sized chunks
- 4oz. bacon or spicy smoked sausage, chopped

1. Arrange the fish steaks in a baking dish and sprinkle with lime juice, tarragon, and salt and pepper.

2. Cover and bake for 15 minutes at 375–400°F or until it is just cooked through.

3. Meanwhile, purée the roasted tomatoes with the salsa in a blender or a food processor. Season with oregano and cinnamon, with extra chipotle if needed. Set the salsa aside.

4. Boil the plantains for 10 minutes or until just cooked through. At the same time, brown the bacon or sausage in its own fat until crispy. Mash the plantains and combine with the bacon or sausage and just enough of its own fat (or olive oil, or butter) to make a smooth, luscious mixture. Season with salt and pepper, and cinnamon or oregano.

5. When the fish is cooked through, remove from the pan and splash it with the puréed tomato salsa. Serve with the mashed plantains.

NUTRITIONAL INFORMATION				
	TOTAL FAT	SAT FAT	CHOL	ENERGY
Total	67.4g	22.5g	259mg	1935kcals
Per Serving	17g	5.5g	65mg	484kcals

PESCADO CON CILANTRO

FISH BAKED WITH LIME AND CILANTRO

SERVES 4

- 2lb. fillets of white fish such as snapper, bass, flounder, or cod
- salt and pepper
- ⅓ cup lime juice
- 3tbsp. olive oil
- 1 large onion, chopped
- 3 cloves garlic, chopped
- 2–3 jalapeños en escabeche, chopped
- 1–2oz. fresh cilantro, coarsely chopped

1. Sprinkle the fish with salt and pepper, then squeeze lime juice all over it.

2. Heat the olive oil in a skillet and fry the onion and garlic until soft and lightly golden.

3. Arrange about a third of the onion mixture and a little of the chilis and cilantro in a baking dish then place the fish on top. Top with the remaining onions, chilis, and cilantro.

4. Bake in a preheated oven at 350°F for about 15 minutes or until the fish has become slightly opaque and firmed. Serve immediately.

NUTRITIONAL INFORMATION				
	TOTAL FAT	SAT FAT	CHOL	ENERGY
Total	40g	5.5g	460mg	1148kcals
Per Serving	10g	1g	115mg	287kcals

BRAISED, STEWED, AND ROASTED DISHES

CAMARONES CON MANGUE
SHRIMP WITH MANGO

Here shrimp are cooked in a brick-red mild chili sauce, then served dotted with bits of sweet mango. Serve with a pile of warm, tender tortillas, and a pitcher of icy fruit and tequila drink.

SERVES 4

1 ancho chili

1 New Mexico or guajilla chili

1 onion, halved but unpeeled

3 cloves garlic, whole and unpeeled

4 fresh or canned tomatoes, diced

dash of ground cinnamon

1–2tbsp. oil

1–1½ cups fish stock

juice of 1 lime

1½lb. shrimp, shelled and cleaned

TO GARNISH

1 mango, peeled and diced

1 fresh red chili such as jalapeño, thinly sliced

1tbsp. chopped fresh cilantro

½ lime, cut into wedges

1. Lightly toast the chilis in an ungreased heavy-based skillet then pour over hot water to cover. Let rehydrate for at least 30 minutes. When softened, remove the stems and seeds, then slice the flesh and purée in a blender or food processor, using just enough soaking liquid to make a smooth paste.

2. Meanwhile, toast the onion and garlic in an ungreased heavy-based skillet until lightly charred.

3. When the onion is cool enough to handle, peel and dice both onion and garlic, then purée with the tomatoes and cinnamon and add to the chili purée.

4. Heat the oil in a skillet, then pour in the purée and cook over medium high heat until it reduces, about 5–8 minutes.

5. Add the stock and simmer until it forms a smooth sauce. Add the lime juice and shrimp. Cook for only 1–2 minutes until the shrimp become pink and opaque. Do not overcook or they will be dry and unpleasant.

6. Serve the shrimp and sauce garnished with mango, red chili, cilantro, and wedges of lime.

NUTRITIONAL INFORMATION

	TOTAL FAT	SAT FAT	CHOL	ENERGY
Total	17g	2.5g	1463mg	844kcals
Per Serving	4g	0.5g	366mg	211kcals

PIPIAN VERDE DE CAMARONES
SHRIMP IN GREEN PUMPKIN-SEED SAUCE

SERVES 4

6oz. pumpkin seeds, shelled but untoasted

1 small or ½ medium onion, chopped

3 cloves garlic, chopped

1–2tbsp. chopped fresh cilantro

12oz. tomatillos, cooked and drained

1–2 chilis such as jalapeño, thinly sliced

½tsp. ground cumin

½tsp. ground coriander

3tbsp. olive oil

1 cup chicken stock

1½lb. shrimp, shelled

2tbsp. lime juice

3 green onions, thinly sliced, to garnish

1. Grind the pumpkin seeds in a spice or coffee grinder then purée in a blender or food processor with the onion, garlic, fresh cilantro, tomatillos, chilis, cumin, and ground coriander.

2. Heat the oil in a skillet then pour in this sauce and cook for about 5 minutes or until it reduces by about a third.

3. Pour in the stock and lower the heat, simmering until the sauce thickens slightly, then add the shrimp and cook only until heated through and opaque pink rather than translucent.

4. Season to taste with lime juice, salt and pepper, and serve sprinkled with green onions.

NUTRITIONAL INFORMATION

	TOTAL FAT	SAT FAT	CHOL	ENERGY
Total	118g	18g	1463mg	1962kcals
Per Serving	30g	4g	366mg	491kcals

INDEX

Index compiled by Sheila Seacroft